A Sailor Rei

1967-1968

Preface

I found myself by myself, wondering if things were supposed to be the way they were. I thought about that concept for a year while I was "in country." It set in motion a whole range of thoughts that took many years to contemplate, flesh out, and ultimately to come to some conclusions.

The turbulent, cultural upheaval called the Anti-War Movement did much to cloud the issue. The idea that we shouldn't be fighting in Vietnam was a point well-taken--one that has been proven true in the years since that debacle ended. However, the government propagated the story that patriotic Americans should support the Johnson administration's war in Vietnam against the Communists. Their story was that the "radical hippie, dope-smoking, commie threat" of the Anti-War Movement was un-American and had no validity during a war. The majority of the United States population sided with the Johnson administration, in the beginning. What later befell trust in that government and its war was serious opposition--Americans lost faith in Lyndon Johnson and his equally corrupt secretary of defense, Robert McNamara. The distrust of Johnson led to his political defeat and came close to destroying the future trust in any American government in the minds of many. The distrust of a government that told us to be quiet and believe them because "they knew best" still exists within the very many of us who went to Southeast Asia.

I have had my trust restored, in part, because of the actions and accomplishments of

President Donald Trump. I believe he is the only American president, in my lifetime, that has stood steadfast in the fight against the corrupt, criminal activity that has been destroying this country since the enactment of the Federal Reserve Act of 1913--it has been a long, drawn-out attack against our nation. President Trump is the first since President Jack Kennedy to actively fight against the deep state and the global cabal, which cares nothing for our individual rights or economic prosperity. His deeds prove that he is sincere when he says he'll never quit fighting for the American people. Therefore, I am encouraged for the first time in many decades. The deep state is losing the battle, and none too soon.

With that background stated, herein is my story about a year in the pathetic and pitiful country of the Republic of Vietnam. I do not speak for anyone other than myself and of my own experiences in a foreign country at war.

As it turned out, because I was an individual replacement, there was no "band of brothers," no comrades in arms, no commitment to each other, no goals to achieve, nor any apparent attempt to "win" the war. I believe we were actually finished before we'd even gotten started because of Johnson's micro-management from the Oval Office--and some few of us knew it back then.

Many ridiculous and often comic events are recorded in this attempt to describe what it was like for me in the hot, humid rain and swirling mist, fire, and smoke of Riverine operations in the Mekong Delta.

Chapter 1

I joined the Naval Reserve in the spring of 1966 to avoid the sure call to report for the draft. That summer, I reported to MCRD, San Diego, California, for reserve boot camp. It was a short course of two weeks, followed by a two-week cruise on a destroyer. We sailed out of San Diego Bay on the USS *Shields*, bound for San Francisco. After a short liberty, we left the Golden Gate for several days of war games, three or four hundred miles out to sea. The intent was for us to operate as the aggressor ship and attempt an attack on a carrier task force. Once darkness fell, the captain had the deck crew rig strings of lights, covered with brown paper bags, along part of the superstructure--the idea was to appear as a tramp freighter with port holes. The ship cruised along at about eight knots, slowly angling for the carrier. Once we closed in on the carrier task force, the captain ordered flank speed, and we made a gun and torpedo run at the ship. We actually achieved our goal and claimed we had shot up the carrier with our five-inch guns. The carrier, for its part, launched a pair of F4 Phantoms and claimed they had blown us out of the water, which was also accurate.

While at sea, we engaged in a drag race with another destroyer--a newer class that was heavier and not nearly as fast as our Fletcher class, reserve ship with its experimental boilers. The bosun's mate said they had actually made well over forty knots on a four-boiler run. We beat the other ship with only two boilers on line.

One day, a heavy sea began to run--the swells reached about fifteen feet. I had been assigned the afterlife buoy watch on the ship's fantail. Having grown up at the beach surfing, I was carefully watching the ship plowing into the sea. It wasn't long before she took green water about four feet deep across the main deck. I saw it coming swiftly down the deck at me, so I jumped onto the aft, five-inch gun mount as the Pacific Ocean rushed by and across the fantail. I called the bridge on the sound-powered phone and let them know I was hanging onto the gun mount. The reply was to secure from my position and report to the bridge. It was to be the first of many experiences of being left to my own devices to survive.

The two-week cruise ended back in San Diego. While we were being pushed to the pier by a tug, the tug captain realized he had us going too fast, sideways--we were about to smash into the pier. He jammed the tug in reverse and added full power. The disastrous result was that the cable he had attached to our ship couldn't stand the strain. I was on deck, forward, and saw what was coming, so before anyone yelled a warning, I scurried around to the other side of the 01 level just as the cable snapped and came slamming across the deck like a scythe. Fortunately, no one was hit by the writhing, slashing cable, but we still crashed into the pier and did some damage to both the pier and the ship.

During the rest of the year, I attended weekly reserve meetings, learning basic electricity. The time came for me to enter active duty, and I was assigned to signalman school in San Diego. It was an eight-week course in which we learned Morse code, flag hoist, semaphore, and how to send messages with flashing light.

I had my car, a 1964 Falcon Sprint, on base and left every day after class for the beach, if the surf was up. If not, four of us would make for Tijuana, Mexico, and the tequila. The aftermath of those evenings made for some very miserable mornings, sitting in class, staring at a twelve-inch searchlight that was blasting our eyeballs out.

The course soon ended, and we were all issued orders. Most of us were headed to Vietnam, one way or another. For my part, I had never been trained for war of any kind, had never fired a gun, and had never been instructed in hand-to-hand combat.

They granted me a couple weeks' leave before I was to fly to Vietnam. My dad and I took a horse-pack trip into the High Sierras for some great times, fishing beautiful lakes for Brook and Golden trout. The trip ended all too quickly, and I found myself reporting to Norton Airforce Base, San Bernardino, California. We loaded up in a C-141 Star Lifter in the middle of the night and took our seats, facing backwards. There were no windows.

Our flight left from Norton and headed to Fort Lewis, Washington; Anchorage, Alaska; and Yokota, Japan, where we de-planed for an hour or so. While there, I was accosted by taunting from soldiers and sailors who were returning to the States. They were calling us "their replacements" and trying to scare us. We were surprised by the verbal abuse but chose to ignore them. I determined to never do such to anyone, no matter what I felt like on my trip home, assuming I made it through the coming year. We loaded back onto the airplane and headed for Da Nang, Vietnam. I have never figured out if the pilot was just screwing around with us or if he was serious, but, halfway to Da Nang, he yelled out over the intercom that we had lost one engine and were having trouble with a second. He told us to prepare to ditch, because we were going down. So, there we were, perhaps going into the South China Sea before even getting close to the war itself. After a few minutes, he came back on the intercom and reported that they had all four engines running smoothly once again.

It was the middle of the night, again, when we stepped out into the fetid, humid air of Vietnam. Our sea bags were thrown into a pile, and we were told to sort them out and get aboard a cattle car. There was one, weak light on a pole, which didn't do much to illuminate the area. The sea bags were dark green, and our black-stenciled names were almost impossible to see. Finally, we clambered into a semitrailer with one side cut away. There were three tiers of benches longways in the van, and we sat looking out into the blackness as the truck hauled us along. While crossing a large bridge, the night suddenly erupted with gunfire and star shells. I didn't know if the Marines guarding the bridge were fooling with us or if there was an actual gunfight going on. A short time later, we arrived at Camp Ten Shaw transit barracks, situated immediately below Monkey Mountain. After grabbing a mattress cover, blanket, and pillow, I entered the barracks and chose a bunk. Out of caution, I chose a middle rack, even before discovering there would be rats on the floor and lizards hanging upside down from the metal-roof ceiling. We were exhausted after the twenty-eight-hour flight. It was September 1, 1967.

In the morning, I headed for the shower and latrine building. Stepping out from the barracks, I immediately had to dodge bullets from a sniper, somewhere up on the mountain above me. I found a toilet and was sitting on the pot when several Vietnamese women entered the latrine and began laughing at me--it did nothing but make me mad. That was the beginning of my education into the culture of South Vietnam. Within a few days I had seen machine gun nests on the corners, concertina wire barricades everywhere, filthy streets, people taking dumps in grave yards, and old women with shiny black teeth. The younger ones had red teeth, which, I found out, was the result of chewing a narcotic called betel nut. There were cooking fires in the muddy, side streets that gave off a reek like an outhouse was on fire. It was hot, 106 degrees, humid, and foul--I never grew used to the smell. In fact, I hated it and still do to this day--they can keep the friggin' tropics.

No one knew a thing about where my ship, the USS *Benewah*, was. I was told that it would probably put into port in Da Nang harbor, so I waited. Before too long, I was appointed night master at arms at the transit barracks. I had the run of the town and only had to be on duty at night. It was my job to "welcome" the marines and sailors, or anyone else for that matter, and to see that they got a bunk. A bright spot in my boring routine was that I could eat at the mess hall at midnight, as long as no one was checking in.

From time to time, the transit base had a night visitor that harassed the guys standing guard on the perimeter--it was an adult orangutan that would pop up in the night, right in the face of a guard, and scare the hell out of him. The base commander had made it very clear that no one was to shoot the ape--if someone did, there would be hell to pay.

I met a guy in the transit barracks who had been assigned to the lighthouse above Da Nang harbor. I visited him a few times, whenever I could hitch a ride up there. On the corner of the road that led to the lighthouse sat a small, white, Buddhist shrine. Behind it, in the bank, was a cave, and scattered around the base of the cave were piles of dog bones. My acquaintance told me he had seen, coming out of the cave, a five-foot monitor lizard. It had reared up on his side of the truck, staring him directly in the face. He left the lizard in the dust and drove up the hill. I never saw the beast, but I didn't doubt the guy's story. The piles of bones were pretty good evidence that some kind of predator was hiding back in the cave.

Oftentimes, a movie would be shown in an outdoor open area within the compound. One night, while sitting with hundreds of sailors and marines, watching the *Ten Commandments*, someone began yelling out my name. He was in the back, yelling as if there was an emergency. It made me think that maybe someone in my family had a problem back home. So, I hustled through the crowd to see what was going on. When I got to him, it turned out to be my good friend from back home, Danny Kerberg. He was wearing a sloppy-looking, army uniform with pant legs that were ridiculously too short-- he looked completely out of place. Da Nang and the I Corps area was pretty much exclusively Marines, Navy, and Airforce--no Army to speak of.

It turned out that Danny was on his way for an R&R in Japan. He had flown in from the army fire base at Pleiku. Danny had somehow found out that I was at Ten Shaw and had come to visit me. He had been in country for eight or nine months and had already taken two R&Rs. I was not at all surprised by his audacity to obtain a third R&R--Danny had always been a scam artist, way back, and he hadn't let being drafted into the army change his methods. I got him situated with a rack, and we headed off to the mess hall for Mid Rats (Midnight Rations). The mess in Da Nang was the only place I ever found decent food in Vietnam-- they even served chocolate cake on a nightly basis.

Danny explained to me the R&R methods he had used on his superiors in Pleiku. The very first time he had been sent out on a night patrol, walking around in the weeds and rice paddies, he had eliminated any future patrols for himself, permanently--as soon as he and his patrol had gotten off the base, he had begun yelling at the top of his lungs. The second lieutenant had ordered him to shut up, but he had proceeded to yell even louder. The patrol returned to the base and he was reported to the next officer in line. The other soldiers agreed they never wanted him on a patrol again. Thereafter, he was ordered to stay in the compound and do other duties. He was with a supply company, so he spent his days either in the warehouse or in a lawn chair on a hill in the middle of the base. He would take a book from the base library and read it for hours. The officers were glad to approve him for R&R, because it got him off the base and away from any other potential malcontents. They simply left him to his own devices, and he made the most of it--that was Danny. And he never changed in his short lifetime--he died at 44 years old playing his favorite sport, basketball.

He and I had a great visit in Da Nang, where we hitchhiked around for five days; then he decided he needed to get some new orders for R&R and asked me the whereabouts of an army base. There wasn't one that I knew of, but there was a small, special ops unit office in town. I waited outside for about an hour, while Danny was inside conning the personnel officer into giving him a full, extra week in Japan. He got a chit for a flight the next day and bumped a bird colonel off the airplane. Off he went to Japan, where he got in a fight with a taxi cab driver. Danny had knocked some teeth out of the cab drivers mouth and had broken his jaw, so he had to go to court. He ended up spending three weeks in Japan before flying back to Vietnam. He spent another week messing around Saigon before finally returning to his unit. All told, he had five weeks of R&R.

One day, I went off to swim and body surf at China Beach, where there were actually some small, two-to-three-foot waves I could drop into. I was having a pretty good time, but it was somewhat disconcerting to look into the water and see banded sea snakes--they seemed to be everywhere. I had been told that, even though they were very poisonous, they were pretty harmless because of their small teeth. Anyway, I was sliding down a wave with my head down to get speed, when I collided with another swimmer--some guy from Pennsylvania who knew nothing about the ocean and had been backing out through the waves, never looking out to the break. We hit hard, and my left eyebrow connected with the back of his skull. I got up and asked him if he was OK, because he was moaning and groaning, holding the back of his head. He said he was alright but asked if I was OK. I said I was fine and turned to dive into the water again, when the vision in my left eye went blurry-- the impact had split my eyebrow with a deep gash. I splashed water on my face, and it ran red, back into the sea. So, I headed for the beach, grabbed my T-shirt, wrapped it around my head, and looked for a ride to the hospital. An Air Force officer picked me up with his jeep and deposited me at a Quonset Hut field hospital.

When I arrived, helicopters were delivering casualties from a fight on the DMZ. The corpsmen brought a stretcher out of a helicopter with a wounded Marine on it--he was on his belly, with three streams of blood pumping out of his back about ten inches high. They were holding plasma and blood containers high as the liquid flowed into the wounded kid, but he was pumping it out as fast as it was flowing in. One of the corpsmen directed me through a door and told me to hang a left when I got through the first building.

I walked into a charnel house--there were about thirty or more men lying on stretchers that were sitting across saw horses. The men were in various stages of destruction, all were dead. I looked into the faces of two or three until I came to a kid of about 19, who was staring up at me with blank eyes--his belly was blown open, and all of his guts were hanging down to the floor. That was enough for me--I had seen all I ever wanted to see. I made for the far door and headed down the hall, where I found a corpsman--he did a good job stitching me up, because the scar has disappeared.

After several weeks of waiting, I figured out that my ship was never going to come into Da Nang. If I was going to get aboard, get a chance at advancement, and complete my year in Vietnam with somebody having a record of my actually being there, I needed to get the ball rolling. I kept checking with them at the personnel office until they finally found my tub in the Mekong Delta. My orders were cut, and I was told to get to the airport and try to hitch a ride south. It was becoming perfectly clear that I was totally on my own--no one knew or cared where the hell I was. I was learning fast, because I had to.

Chapter 2

I boarded an old-fashioned DC-3, known in the military as a C-47. We left Da Nang for a small city down the coast named Quinon. From there we flew on to Saigon, landing in the dark. I had no idea of where to stay, so I asked around and was directed to the army transit barracks. It turned out to be a complete dump with open latrines. Somehow, I got a ride out to the airport the next day and managed to find a STOL aircraft that was going to the Army/Navy base at Dong Tam. We flew over the delta and its jungle and rice paddies for a while; then the pilot turned the plane on its side, and we began to spiral down to what looked like a small, black helicopter pad. He held the plane in a tight spiral all the way to the very last second, then he leveled the wings, and we hit the deck. He slammed the brakes on and reversed the props as we rushed down the "runway" and stopped. When he turned the plane around, a wing tip brushed the trees at the end of the runway. It was a helicopter pad after all-- made of expanded-metal, interlocking panels laid over the red dirt of the delta. I grabbed my sea bag and stepped out the rear ramp. No sooner had the eighteen of us begun making our way towards a building on the far side of the helicopter pad than artillery started going off, causing us to jump and run for cover. But we figured out soon enough that is was outgoing, 155mm, howitzer rounds, aimed south over the river.

My heart sank when I got a good look at the ugly, green, smoke-stained ships anchored in the muddy Mekong. They were absolutely the worst-appearing collection of filthy scum, barge-looking excuses for navy ships I had ever seen. If there was ever a unit that looked like it had been to hell and had not returned, it was this motley mess of old, WWII, converted LSTs. They were designated APBs with an ARL, acting as a tender and repair ship--I will describe them fully a little later.

I jumped down into the Admin boat, a WWII style, Mike boat that had been used in amphibious landings. Most of us have seen them in WWII documentaries, landing Army and Marines on beaches. Anyway, off it lumbered, spewing diesel smoke, towards the barracks ship, USS *Benewah*. There were two, large barges tied along one side that served as a mooring for the boats and as a utility space for loading and unloading troops and equipment. Shortly after reporting aboard, I was informed that I was to be TAD (Temporary Assigned Duty) to the *Askari*, which was an ARL, a repair ship. The following day, I rode the Admin boat to the *Askari* and reported aboard. Someone in the personnel office told me to find a bunk in a certain compartment forward on the starboard side. I had nothing else to do that day since I was the new guy, so I chose a middle rack, found a locker, and stowed my gear. I decided to write a letter to my parents to let them know I had finally found my ship.

There was no one else in the compartment, so I settled down on my stomach, with my pillow propping me up, to write. I was into the second or third page of the letter when the hatch opened, and a big, black guy stepped through and dogged the hatch. He never said a word as he lay down on the bottom, unused bunk, right below me. He lay there for a minute and then began to push his foot up against the thin, canvas rack and mattress, right into my stomach. Once, twice, thrice did he push. I had grown up having to deal with bullies from time to time, so I knew that if I didn't do something, my time aboard that tub was going to be pure hell. There was nothing else for it but to take charge immediately and finish his game before it developed into something worse. After that third push, I rolled over the side and shoved my government, ballpoint pen into his throat, right below the Adam's apple. I pushed hard and pinned him to the canvas with the pen, poised to ram it through his neck. Then I warned him to never, ever touch me again, because, if he did, I would kill him. I kept the pressure on the pen, while he turned from black to purple. Before removing the pen, I got a promise from him to leave me alone, forever. He gasped for air, clambered off the bunk, and got the hell out of the compartment.

At that time, there was quite a bit of racial tension in the Navy. That black guy evidently let his other friends know about me, because I was never bothered again by anyone on board. I found out from a couple of people that he was supposed to be the "baddest bastard" on board the *Askari*--I could have cared less. I never bothered anyone, and I sure as hell never wanted anyone to bother me. I saw him all the time after that, and we always exchanged strained greetings. I got along with some other black guys that were in a Judo class that we had on board. My signalman chief was black. It didn't matter to me what color they were, as long as they left me be.

During those first few weeks, when I was adjusting to life aboard a repair craft, I began to study for advancement to E-4, third class, petty officer. I wanted the promotion in rank for a couple of reasons: a raise in pay and a little more privilege, small as it was.

One of the chief petty officers ordered some gym mats, and several of us enrolled in his Judo classes. I enjoyed the workout and the few moves I learned that I thought might actually come in handy if we had a hand to hand with the VC.

On one of my first night watches, a shot rang out from the quarter deck. The officer of the deck told me to stand by as he went below to investigate. I thought we might have been boarded by swimmers trying to attack the ship while it was asleep. There was a gun cabinet in the pilot house (conn), but it was locked, and I didn't know where the key was. So, I grabbed two, heavy, brass belaying pins from the flag bag on the signal bridge and hunkered down behind the hatch. Finally, the OD returned and told me that someone had shot himself in the head, committing suicide, because of a "Dear John" letter he had received from his wife. He had only had a few weeks to go before he was to leave Vietnam. Despair is a terrible thing, but shooting himself because his wife was unfaithful was, I thought, ridiculous. The OD asked about the belaying pins in my hands, and I told him what my plan had been--he just shook his head. Well, I knew that I wasn't about to stand around and wait for some VC, night visitor to stab or shoot me without a fight.

We had a small contingent of UDT (Underwater Demolition Team) aboard the ship that ran recon patrols into the canals, before they launched amphibious operations with the Army. The UDT would ride a water scooter, a type of   pre-WaveRunner, up the canals, blow bridges, and scout out landing zones (LZs). One day, I was down on the barges moored alongside the ship, when one of the UDT men held up an eleven-foot python his buddies had killed on their latest excursion upriver. Driving those water scooters around in the dark looked like no fun, as far as I was concerned. They lay on them and trailed their legs in the water, and the river was a sewer from China, containing all manner of filth. It was also home to crocs, poisonous snakes, and river rats. Several times I even saw dead, human bodies floating down the river at low tide.

Before life on the river, I had never eaten eggs or drunk coffee. But shortly after boarding the *Askari*, I began partaking of both, out of necessity. On the ship, our food was terrible, but, comparatively speaking, the powdered eggs were edible. The filthy river water had been run through desalters and made into Kool-Aid, but I drank the coffee, because the water had been boiled at least twice. Whenever I was able to get over to Dong Tam, I'd buy cases of unsweetened grapefruit juice from the PX. I kept the juice cold, stored in the top of the air conditioner in my compartment. By the way, the compartment was a berth for 18 men, measuring about eight feet wide and twenty-plus feet long. There were banks of lockers in between the six-foot racks, and the overhead was not quite seven feet high. Since I was six foot two and a half, my feet always stuck out the bottom of my rack. There were no portholes in the hull, the air conditioners were the only source of oxygen for all 18 of us. We could not sleep down there if the mechanics needed power to repair the boats-- they would shut off the air conditioners, and the compartment would go to one-hundred- fifty degrees in minutes, with no oxygen to breathe. I would retreat to the after-part of the signal bridge and sit upright in a chair, trying to sleep, which was made nearly impossible by the incessant insects and rain.

Speaking of insects, they were everywhere, oversized, and a constant nuisance. During the monsoon rains, flying insects would die by the hundreds and fall to the deck at night. I had to scoop them up in a dust pan, shovel them into a bucket, and dump them over the side before I could swab the deck every morning. They had orange and black striped bodies that were about two and a half inches long with wingspans about four inches wide. Once, while going up a ladder to the top of the conn, I came face to face with a large praying mantis-- it was about eight inches long. And, of course, the mosquitoes were a constant irritant. We had to take malaria pills every week to avoid contracting Yellow Fever.

One day, my friend, Mike, and I got a chance to get off our respective ships and go over to Dong Tam. It was a combination Army/Navy base that had a large-turning basin for the boats. A brigade of the Ninth Infantry Division of the Army was based there.

Whenever we got underway for an amphibious assault, we would embark the Army on board the barracks ships and load them into the ATCs. An ATC was a converted Mike boat with two-foot-thick, dense foam along the hull and the con, overlaid with 5/8 rebar, spaced every two inches horizontally--the rebar was intended to stop rockets from penetrating the hull and the conn. An ATC was armed with three-gun tubs located on the stern. The turrets held two, .50 caliber machine guns and a 20mm cannon. ATCs were also equipped with mine-sweeping gear, because the VC were very fond of planting anti-ship mines that they would float downriver at low tide. Since we were in a tidal river, the current could reach six knots as the water ran out to sea on an ebb tide. Floating with the tide was a lot of riverine vegetation, perfect for hiding mines. One night, fourteen men were wounded and seven killed with a mine, just upriver from us.

The ATC had a waterproof, canvas cover over the well deck to keep rain and sun off the troops as they rode into battle. When they arrived at their destination, the ramp would drop, and the soldiers would charge into the jungle, just like the WWII, amphibious landings in the Pacific.

Anyway, Mike and I got what we wanted at the PX on the base and walked across the dusty, red-dirt compound to a giant, black-rubber, above-ground, swimming pool the Army had installed. Next to the pool were round, metal, patio tables with umbrellas, where we could sit and drink San Miguel beer from the Philippines--it was a hundred times better than the rotten beer we got every six weeks, or so, aboard the barges. We changed into our swimming trunks and dove right into the pool. The water wasn't actually refreshing, since it was in the 90-degree-plus range, but at least it was wet.

We were swimming laps when, suddenly, the VC launched an intense mortar attack upon the base. They were dropping their huge, 120mm mortars all over the place, so we scrambled out of the water as fast as we could. We ran across the blazing-hot sand for the nearest bunker, which was above ground and eight feet high, with double, ¾-inch plywood walls, two feet apart, filled with sand. The roof was made of reinforced plywood, with several layers of sandbags above to absorb the mortars. We raced up to the bullfighter-style door of the bunker and were faced with dozens of Vietnamese women piled on top of each other, all screaming and crying. In our panic to get away from the mortar barrage, we began trying to pull women out of the bunker to make room for ourselves. Then I came to my senses, realized what was going on, and yelled for Mike to head for the other end of the base where there was another bunker. The women were probably employees of the PX, and some may have been whores that operated a cat-house near the base entrance.

We began a sizzling, three-hundred-yard dash towards the other bunker. In the process, the ammunition dump was blown up, and all manner of ordinance began to explode--that conflagration was entirely too close for comfort. When a mortar landed close to us, we zigged and zagged as we crossed the burning sand, hoping we wouldn't get hit with shrapnel.

Then I saw a red flare go off above the base, indicating the VC were coming through the wire and trying to rush the base. We were unarmed and practically naked--it was not a good situation, so I ran like a gazelle for safety. Rushing towards the bunker entrance, I angled for the narrow space behind the front section that protected the opening from hostile fire. I left the ground in a headlong leap, stretched out, flew into the bunker, and splatted into the muddy depression at the entrance. Mike followed, landing on top of me; he, too, was covered with the rank, stinking mud.

I looked up and saw six Korean marines laughing at us practically-naked, mud-caked Americans. The ROK (Republic of Korea) marines wore multiple hand-grenades, extra clips for their M-16s, and large, fighting knives over their camo uniforms. Right away I knew that no VC was going to survive trying to get into that bunker while those guys were in there. We grinned at them, and they offered us beer. Together, eight of us waited out the attack until the "all clear" was sounded.

Our little shopping, swimming trip turned out alright in the end, but the middle part was pretty exciting. The VC had gotten lucky and had dropped a mortar square onto the one-and-only bar that had served good beer--that oasis was never rebuilt. The ammunition dump they had hit, while we were dodging the mortars, continued to blow up for another twenty-four hours. Mike and I caught the Admin boat back to our respective ships and showered to wash off the slime and mud.

It turned out that the American Armed Forces' local newspaper, the *Stars and Stripes*, ran an article weekly that reported about mortar attacks on U.S. bases. Dong Tam and the base at Khe San, on the DMZ, vying for the most-mortared bases in all of South Vietnam. It was not a record that anyone was particularly fond of. Additionally, the VC would regularly attempt to drop mortars on the ships, particularly during the night.

One night, while standing watch on the signal bridge, I was sitting on the edge of the flag bag. I saw the fire from the shot of the mortar on the south bank and then, of course, saw nothing. Suddenly, the mortar fell, literally right next to me about a foot off my right shoulder, and exploded in the water about twenty feet below where I sat. That was too close for my blood, but there was nothing to do about it because it was a lone shot. We didn't even go to general quarters, there was really nothing to fight. Most of the nights while on watch we were sniped at. We were likely targets with white T-shirt's on, especially if the snipers had a night scope illuminating us. It was a regular occurrence to have their bullets ricochet around the mast and stanchions of the twenty-four-inch, searchlight platform. They would usually shoot just once every hour or so. No one was ever hit on our ship. I don't know if anyone on the other ships ever got shot.

Chapter 3

The south bank of the river was about half a mile or farther from our usual anchorage off of Dong Tam. As I mentioned, it was often the place from which they lobbed mortars. The Dong Tam base regularly got hit from the north side of the perimeter. Several times a week, intense mortar fire would erupt during the middle of the night, directed against the base. There was a contingent of Navy, Sea Wolf helicopters based at Dong Tam. They were Huey gunships that mounted miniguns and rocket pods. Typically, two of them would take off, one with his running lights on and the other with them off. They would circle around to the location of the VC mortar men. Then the chopper, with its red and green lights on, would decoy the VC and draw fire from their position. The VC ammunition had orange tracers; ours were red. We would see an orange stream of tracers reaching up for the decoy chopper, when, suddenly, the night sky would erupt with a barrage of rockets from the other Sea Wolf, pummeling the mortar position--which would be the end of that mortar crew. The VC never seemed to figure out our tactics, probably because there were no survivors left to tell the tale. Time and again, the same nighttime scenario was repeated. The choppers would land, and the crews would standby in case of another attack. But that was not the norm--the usual attack was but once a night.

The south bank was known, VC territory. Whenever we had a serious mortar or rocket attack from there, an air strike would launch from one of the Airforce bases near Saigon the following day. It would typically consist of two F-100 fighter bombers. Each plane would target mud bunkers and other VC installations with two, five-hundred-pound bombs, four, two-hundred-and-fifty-pound bombs, some cluster bombs, and then run all of their 20mm cannon rounds against the targets. If they ever did any real damage, we never noticed, but it was a good show, and the pilots had fun. Once empty of ordinance, they would scream off upriver and out of sight. Then they would turn around and come downriver, just off the water, aimed right at the ships. Both pilots would stand their jets on their tails and hit the burners, going straight up above our masts. It broke the monotony, and we always had hope they had killed some VC.

While the year of 1967 waned, the mortar attacks picked up from the south bank. We began moving up and down the delta as a unit, the Army assaulting supposed-VC strongholds, while we transported and supported them. Nothing really significant occurred besides some firefights with the boats and the ever-present VC attempting ambushes close to the river banks and in the canals. After a certain operation, the MRF (Mobile Riverine Force) returned to its anchorage off of Dong Tam. The ships were in their usual configuration, anchored about five hundred yards apart, with the major force of ATCs and Monitors tied up to the barges. The mortar attacks increased and continued for several nights in a row from the south bank of the river.

One day, a boat deposited three, VC prisoners and two, strange-looking, black-pajama-clad Americans on one of our barges. I was looking down from the signal bridge, trying to figure out what was going on. The UDT guys walked over and began talking with the pajama-clad Americans, who were also wearing Vietnamese-style, conical straw hats. It was an odd-looking group, with the three VC just sitting there on a packing box. I finished my watch, descended the ladder, and walked down the brow to the barge--I wanted a closer look at the group. The VC prisoners looked back at me with wild-eyed terror--I think they were actually shuddering. When I turned around, I looked right into the eyes of a pasty-white, skinny, short, little, American SEAL. His eyes looked like the rattlesnakes I had seen while growing up in Southern California--they were absolutely dead, like there was no soul in there. His buddy had the same build and eyes--it gave me the creeps. If I remember right, the SEALS reported aboard our ship, and then were gone within the hour, taking their terrified prisoners with them. I never saw another SEAL while in Vietnam, that I know of. The story I got from the UDT men was that the VC had set up a mortar position and had zeroed in on the ships. The SEALS had slithered up on them in the night and lopped off the heads of two with their garrotes. Then they had brought the remaining three back to the MRB (Mobile Riverine Base) to interrogate. The killers in the black pajamas were small, dressed like Vietnamese peasants or VC, and blended in perfectly, except for their pasty-white skin.

They were not heavily muscled, but I was sure they were wire-tough, deadly, killing machines that would stick a knife in someone at the slightest provocation. They truly resembled the grim reaper himself.

We had a continual patrol of two boats circling the ships, on the lookout for mines and/or san-pans slipping within our large perimeter. They would randomly toss concussion grenades at seaweed floating among the ships, in case a mine might be concealed within the vegetation. They were supposed to interdict any native boats within the perimeter, but the natives may or may not have known about our rules. The usual practice was to inspect the san-pans and check for any contraband, weapons, or personnel aboard that might be the enemy. Of all the san-pans I saw, they just carried farmers or families going about their business up and down the river. On this day, a particularly-idiotic fool was at the helm of one of our ninety-ton boats, flying a Confederate flag below the American flag. Without warning, he sped up close to a low-lying san-pan, causing it to almost capsize from the wake of the boat. Then he pulled his boat into reverse and backed down right over the Vietnamese, little, wooden boat. The occupants were thrown under his sixty-foot boat, and they came up sputtering and screaming--they were all women except for a twelve-year-old boy. He surfaced a couple of minutes later, dead by drowning. This incident occurred right next to our barge. Some of our crew hauled the kid out of the water, and our corpsman rushed down to the barge to try to save him, but to no avail. There was instant rage in our crew, and particularly with the UDT contingent. The Confederate-flag-flying idiot was ordered away from our ship, and later he was reported by a witness to the command ship, the USS *Benewah*. I hope the bastard got sent to Leavenworth Prison, but I never heard what actually happened to him. That he had committed murder was evident to anyone who had witnessed the incident.

This would be a good time to describe which vessels made up the Mobile Riverine Force, known as Riverine Assault Force 117. There were two APBs, the *Benewah*, and the *Colleton*. They were WWII, LST hulls, configured for berthing Army troops. The *Benewah* was the command ship of the flotilla. They sported two decks above the main deck with a helicopter landing platform behind the forward bridge. They were armed with 40mm, quad mount, anti-aircraft, rapid-fire cannon, fore and aft, and two, slow-fire, three-inch guns that could reach out ten miles. The Benewah gunners on the three-inch rifles were good shots. I once saw them shoot a three-inch projectile right through the front door of a hut and out the back wall. It didn't explode but kept right on going into the jungle--this was while the ship was moving upriver. There were various .50 caliber machine gun mounts on the super structure. My ship, the *Askari*, still had the regular configuration of the rear-mounted conn and bridge that standard LSTs had. We also had Quad-forty, anti-aircraft guns, fore and aft. The quad means they had four barrels that were loaded with eight-shell clips, which sported two-inch-diameter bullets. They were usually high-explosive rounds that could chop down big trees in seconds. The clips were dropped into the guns as fast as the loaders could move. For an example, check out any WWII ship fighting against Japanese aircraft, and you'll see the forties in action. We also had an APL, which was towed by a tug boat. The APL was a multi-deck, barracks barge that could house scores of troops. I never went aboard it and have no idea if she had guns or not. The fifth ship in our force consisted of a modern (at that time) fleet LST. She was much larger than our dirty, green tub and was actually painted haze-grey, like a Navy ship should be. She was our primary fuel, ammunition, and stores-supply ship and rotated every three months with another fleet LST. She mounted six, rapid-fire, three-inch guns, capable of firing sixty rounds a minute per barrel. Those were the support ships for the flotilla. Another old LST from the fleet would make regular runs upriver to supplement the supply of the flotilla.

The assault force consisted of ATCs, Monitors, and ASPBs. By the early part of 1968, that force numbered about one hundred, riverine, assault boats. The ATC, as described earlier, transported the Army when we launched assaults against the VC.

A Monitor was a converted Mike boat with the same kind of bar armor and dense foam along the hull and encasing the conn as an ATC. It was equipped with the three turrets, or gun tubs, on the stern like the ATC's had--two 50's and a 20mm gun. The ramp and large well deck were gone and in place was a sealed bow with a large turret that housed a 40mm cannon and a .50 caliber machine gun. Behind the turret was a smaller well deck, armed with .30 caliber machine guns at the four corners of the well. In the middle of the well was an 82mm mortar. The fan tail sported the usual mine-sweeping gear.

Eventually, two of the Monitors had their forward guns removed and replaced with dual directional, ten-inch-wide nozzles that spewed a stream of napalm about a hundred yards. There were high-pressure pumps and a large, fuel bladder placed in the well deck. That configuration was nicknamed a Zippo.

When it became obvious that the VC would stand and fight against guns, particularly during an amphibious assault, the decision was made to stop the heavy casualties inflicted upon our sailors and soldiers during these operations-- hence the Zippo. None of the enemy was about to stick around shooting RPG-7s and AK-47s when the canal banks, one hundred yards inland on each side, were set ablaze. The Zippos pretty well ended the surprise attacks while landing troops.

The ASPB was a lightly-armored boat that was built for the specific task of supporting riverine operations. From what I could tell, it was a death trap whenever the VC fired rockets into its superstructure. Our corpsman had to scrape dead sailors off the inside of the superstructure more than once when an ASPB returned to the *Askari* for battle-damage repair. It would look like a tin can after a cherry bomb had gone off inside it.

While I was there, we did not operate with the Swift Boats. They were usually found operating closer to the sea along the lower reaches of the river deltas and the coast itself.

PBRs were used for various tasks but were typically involved with the support and transport of SEALS and South Vietnamese troops.

As 1967 came to a close, our operations began to increase. But we were not prepared for what was about to occur across the entire country.

Sometime around the end of the year, a force of C-130 airplanes came thundering down the south bank of the river across from where we were anchored. I counted thirty of them in a staggered line, dumping agent orange on the jungle. Fortunately for us, the wind was prevailing north to south, and the mist and fog of the chemicals drifted away from our flotilla. I'm sure this fiasco was more of the lame-brained ideas of McNamara and his "whiz-kids" in the Johnson administration. So, the jungle turned brown after a while; then the monsoon rains came, and the jungle turned green again. This was yet another looney scheme to try something to supposedly win the war, which, of course, never worked.

I had established a routine of avoiding any extra working parties after I had made third class petty officer. They were not supposed to involve me in any menial tasks that were given to those of lesser rank--but they did anyway. I suspected that the second-class signalman and the chief signalman were often volunteering me for those duties. So, whenever I was not on watch but had become aware of something afoot, I would retreat to a secret spot I had found to get out of sight.

On the stern of our ship was an anchor, below which was a platform—it was strong and wide and a perfect place on which to climb down out of sight from anyone above. I had discovered a fishing rod somewhere aboard the ship, so I would stop in the mess decks and grab a chunk of the inedible lunch meat for bait. Then I would carefully pick my time and quietly disappear down below, under the fantail. Fishing for Mekong catfish could be pretty good, if the patrol boats didn't heave a concussion grenade off the stern of the ship. Whenever I caught one of those silver and blue fish, up to twenty pounds, I'd drop it off at the mess deck. I would never eat one of them, since they were subsisting on the foulest food off the bottom of the river, but there were guys that loved catfish and ate them right up.

I had become the librarian and had gotten the key to the ship's library, so I'd play my favorite tapes on the library's reel-to-reel tape deck or spend as much time as possible reading in there. The only problem down in that part of the ship was the regular explosions of the concussion grenades, because the ship's hull conducted the sounds of the explosions very sharply--right into the library.

Chapter 4

Just before January 31st of 1968, a couple of us got a chance to get some "in-country R&R" in Vung Tau, a seaside resort of sorts. I had heard that the VC used to frequent the place at the same time the Americans did. It was supposedly known to each side that there was to be no fighting in the resort. A couple other guys and I rode the old, gator, supply LST downriver to the port of Vung Tau. We had just gotten off the ship and were attempting to see what kind of trouble we could get into, when the Shore Patrol showed up and ushered us back aboard the ship--we had no idea what was going on. We certainly did not want to be stuck aboard that old tub when we could be ashore raising hell like any regular sailor should.

In a short time, we got word that the entire country was under a massive attack--it came to be known as the Tet Offensive. The Viet Cong were simultaneously attacking, by the tens of thousands, across the length of the entire country. American and South Vietnamese bases, units, and strongholds were being overrun and set ablaze. It was a concerted, well-planned offensive that took American forces totally by surprise. The results were devastating for the Viet Cong, and the casualties of Americans mounted with each day of the fight. Tens of thousands of Viet Cong died along with thousands of Americans. The war in Viet Nam had reached its moment of truth.

We hung around Vung Tau for a couple days while the LST loaded up supplies, then put to sea to head back up the Mekong River to the Mobile Riverine Force. That particular LST captain, a Lieutenant, had a penchant for flying a huge American flag from the yardarm--he used large, helium balloons tied to the flag to keep it in the air. The idea was to draw fire from the river bank so his ship could open up on the VC. Nothing happened while I was aboard, riding back upriver to the flotilla. But, the crew told me they got into some pretty good shootouts from time to time--I bet they did.

Before we reached the anchorage off Dong Tam, we began to see large columns of black smoke above the cities of the delta. We passed My Tho, afire, and could see smoke coming from the location of Vin Long, upriver. The fight was on, and the Mobile Riverine Force was in the thick of it. The army was embarked aboard the ATCs and sent into battle for the city of My Tho. Artillery barges were pulled up and secured to the bank in various places. They mounted two, 105 Howitzers on each barge, which were used to give support to the ground troops as they fought for control of the cities. The Sea Wolf helicopters were used to support the artillery. One night while I was on watch off My Tho, a force of VC attempted to overrun an artillery barge and the platoon of soldiers protecting it. I could hear the fight on our ship's radio, while I watched the tracers flying back and forth in the jungle off our starboard side. Some VC had thrown a satchel charge onto the barge, killing part of the gun crew. The army platoon leader called for a chopper to lay down fire on the attackers. I saw the Sea Wolf come in and begin to use its rockets, blasting down at the supposed force of VC. Suddenly, the platoon leader began screaming to get the damned helicopter off of his position. A mistake by the helicopter pilot had targeted the army platoon. The screaming continued for a few seconds as the helicopter sent rockets down upon the army patrol. Then there was an abrupt end of contact with the platoon leader. I don't know how many of our people died in that incident, but the term "friendly fire" is a euphemism that does not describe the carnage that happened. Platitudes about things that "just happen in war", and other such rubbish from people who have no idea what happens in a situation like that, should never be expressed. They are nothing but excuses, and stupid ones at that. In such cases, the ignorant need to keep their mouths shut.

The VC were all around the Dong Tam base, attempting to overrun the place. Our ship moved from one location to another, supporting the force and repairing the boats that had gotten shot up. Sometime later, I heard from a boat crewman that, when his boat had transited the canal that led into the turning-basin at Dong Tam, he had seen the heads of six whores who had worked at the cat-house just off of the base, displayed on pikes along the canal. The VC were masters at many forms of terrorism in their attempt to keep the local population under control.

The PBRs of Task Force 116 and the SEALS engaged the VC that had overrun My Tho. When the MRF arrived in force, the battle became one of pushing the VC units out and securing the city. Supposedly, hundreds of VC were killed in this fight--the concept of measuring success in war by counting bodies was used extensively in Vietnam. It was a worthless, crude attempt to convince the American public, and anyone else who might listen, that we were winning. In truth, it was nothing but bullshit substituted for genuine victory. Time and again, government propaganda were used in an attempt to justify a fiasco and put a successful face on a lie and a losing cause.

The MRF engaged the VC in the city of Vinh Long and crushed the VC forces within two days. A full movement of the MRF to the City of Can Tho was undertaken to counter a threatened attack by 2,500 VC. It took most of the day to transit upriver towards Cambodia, turn into a crossover branch, and sail down the Bassac River to the city. The MRF secured Can Tho from the VC threat and used gunfire from the ships and boats to support the army sweeps of the jungle and surrounding countryside.

When the MRF pulled out for the crossover and the trip back down the main branch of the Mekong, the *Askari* remained on station for a couple of hours. I never knew why we did not go with the rest of the flotilla, but we didn't. Eventually, we got under way and headed upriver for the crossover. Tethered to one of the barges were two Boston Whalers-- fiberglass runabouts with outboard motors.

One of the Boston Whalers broke loose from her mooring and drifted off behind the barge as we moved upriver at about five knots. We had two Monitors along as escorts, one of which moved to secure the loose boat, only to come under withering fire from the north bank. She got the boat tied off and sped up to the security of our ship's guns. The VC were apparently shadowing our movement, waiting for anything that would give them an advantage in an ambush.

Not far upriver from the ambush incident, while we were steaming along, I saw a huge rocket come flying at us from the north bank of the Bassac. It looked to be about the size of a standard telephone pole. The massive projectile came right at our ship and crossed over our mast, about twenty feet up. It was spewing fire and smoke and making a real racket. Thankfully, it missed our ship and continued out into the jungle. I lost sight of it and never did hear an explosion. I have no idea how they got such a huge rocket down into the delta, but several of us speculated they had trucked it down or had strapped it to the back of an elephant. That it had come down the Ho Chi Min trail was obvious.

The traffic on that infamous trail had increased several-fold after Lyndon Johnson called for a bombing halt on the trail and points north. His egotistical, micro-management of the war from the Oval Office was directly responsible for untold thousands of American deaths.

Continuing our movement, we entered the crossover branch and transited to the main Mekong. Just as the current of the river began to push us along, our primary steering gear failed, and we were rudderless in the stream. The captain called down the voice tube to after-steering and ordered it to take control--

his call went unanswered. Several times he yelled for after-steering to take control, when, finally, a voice drifted back up. The guy down there was obviously confused and knew nothing about his job. I knew who he was--a laundry man, who had never been called upon in a dire emergency. Most likely he was asleep down there in the bowels of the ship. Once the captain understood that someone was actually there, he gave orders to steer a course. There was a pregnant silence, and the captain was not happy about it. He yelled down and, once again, ordered after-steering to steer a "such-and such" course. After another drawn-out pause, a voice drifted back up the tube with a response, "Aye, aye, sir."

The ship immediately turned hard to port and rushed at the jungle-covered bank. There was no way to avoid it, as the *Askari* plowed up the bank, crashing through jungle trees and vines and coming to rest with about a hundred and fifty feet of the ship high and dry. The fo'c'sle was strewn with brush and limbs, and monkeys were jumping about the main deck. We immediately went to general quarters to repel boarders, breaking out all the small arms aboard. I had my usual, worthless BAR, but some of the other guys had shotguns and M16s. The captain began ordering the snipes in the engine compartment to back down with one screw, then another, alternating back and forth and working the ship off the muddy bank. It was successful, and we swung back out into the river, turning one three-hundred-sixty-degree circle after another. Finally, when they got the steering gear operational again, we were able to straighten out and make headway. It could have been dicey if those VC who had been dogging our progress had been hidden along that bank when we had crashed into the mud. That incident was not all that unusual for the *Askari*--it seemed that strange misadventures dogged our existence all too often.

The fighting continued throughout the year of 1968. Sometime during those operations, while we were anchored off Dong Tam, we were suddenly infested with rats aboard the ship. At first, the ship's carpenter's shop began reloading shotgun shells with wood chips, so as not to ricochet lead pellets off the steel deck while our personnel took shots at the rats. Evidently, the other ships in the flotilla were experiencing the same problem. Ten tons of Decon rat poison was ordered out of a supply depot, somewhere in-country, and was brought upriver on a tug. Before the Decon arrived, the rat infestation grew steadily worse. Along with the rats, there were discovered poisonous snakes aboard which had, apparently, come to eat the rats. Someone figured out that the brow from the ship to the barges was the route taken by the rats and snakes to get aboard. So, to interrupt their path, the brow was raised at night.

One night, during another siege by the river rats and snakes, I climbed the ladder from my compartment to the main deck to go on watch. When my eyes came level with the main deck, the moonlight revealed hundreds of rats scurrying across the ship--the deck was literally moving. That was the last time I used the main deck to go up to the bridge at night. I immediately descended the ladder and went through the compartments until I could ascend to the bridge from the interior of the ship.

The whole of the MRF was in one, offensive operation after another during those months after the first of February. We got very little sleep because of the necessity of keeping the boats in repair. The hard use and frequent battle damage kept our mechanics, shipfitters, and welders working day and night. We would often come under mortar and rocket fire in the middle of the night. Consequently, tempers were short, and there was increasing animosity amongst the crew.

Chapter 5

During one of those days on the river, I remember a B-52 strike that occurred close to the MRF. We were anchored during full daylight when, suddenly, a massive rumble began upriver. I couldn't tell where the strike was hitting, but the intensity and duration were impressive. I have no idea how many bombers there were, but the strike lasted for several minutes. They were probably hitting a section of the Ho Chi Min trail and its convoys of material and men coming down from North Vietnam. We never got word about the bombing raid, but I could sense how powerful it was—the results must have been devastating.

Sometime later that year, an incident occurred that proved how effectively we were hurting the VC forces in the delta. Word was relayed to us that we had been the target of a North Vietnamese air strike. No plane had ever gotten close enough to shoot at the MRF, but if they had, it would have been a slaughter. It seems that two Migs had taken off from a North Vietnamese airfield somewhere beyond the DMZ. They crossed into Cambodia and descended to low-level flight, just above the river. Radar installations had picked up the Migs as soon as they lifted off in North Vietnam. The Airforce scrambled two, F-4 Phantom fighters to intercept the Migs. They were actually not that far upriver from us when they were shot out of the sky by the Phantoms' missiles--a good end to a very real, potential disaster. Our ship was the secondary fuel and ammunition carrier for the flotilla, and I slept right above a 30,000-gallon tank of JP-5 fuel. If those Migs had attacked our ship, it would have literally blown sky high. We never knew a thing about it until it was all over, but, when we did find out, it gave us pause to contemplate our tenuous existence there on the river.

One day while I was on watch, our deck patrol spotted a VC swimmer attempting to attach some kind of mine to our ship's hull. I saw the deck patrolman heave several concussion grenades over the side and yell for someone to call our patrol boats. Two Monitors rushed to our side and began hurling concussion grenades all around our ship for several minutes. I surmised that no one could sustain such a barrage and live--it was far too intense. Many people were watching the water for a body to float to the surface, which was wishful thinking, since the river had a strong current with occasional, large whirlpools. A dead man would likely float up somewhere quite a distance downriver, if at all. Any number of forces efficiently disposed of the bodies, like crocodiles, giant catfish, rats, crabs, and bacteria. The river was about sixty feet deep in most places, and it was up to a couple miles across. If someone went in, he had better be a very good swimmer, or he would likely be sucked under and disappear. The flotilla had periodic "man overboard" events, but no one was ever found, to my knowledge.

I had been sitting on the wing of the bridge, up on the railing, peering through the big eye, fifty-power binoculars that were mounted on the railing. For some reason, I thought that if the swimmer had survived the onslaught of grenades, he would have made for the south bank and VC-held territory. Suddenly, he came into my view--he had removed his swim fins and was clambering up the riverbank in full view, over half a mile away. He must have had his ear drums blown out by the concussion as well as possible internal injuries from the grenades. But, he had made the bank--quite a feat of survival and strenuous swimming. I figured him to be very lucky to have survived the snakes and crocs during his escape.

One day, I noticed a new, boat crewman walking around on one of our barges. He was dressed in a non-regulation manner and was sporting a huge Bowie knife on one hip. He struck me as a poser, and I mentioned him to a quartermaster friend of mine on the bridge. We both agreed that he was some kind of yahoo. We watched him get aboard one of the Monitors before it headed off to another ship. Several weeks later, that same boat was pulling up to our port side in order to tie off to another boat moored alongside the barge. In such instances, it was required to unload all guns before arriving--there were standing orders to do so.

A single shot rang out, right after they had tied off. That same fool with the Bowie knife had pulled the trigger on one of the .30 caliber machine guns, which still held a round in the breach. The bullet crossed over to the other boat, entered the leg of a crewman, hit his knee, turned up, and shot through his skull, killing him instantly. The victim had only two weeks left of his one-year tour of duty before he was to head home. The careless idiot was arrested and shipped off for court martial. He was lucky the dead man's boat crewmen didn't shoot him right then and there.

During a lull in operations, we would sometimes get a break on a Sunday. About once every six or eight weeks, the captain would order fifty cases of beer, iced down, and those of us not on watch could go to the barges to drink. We would try to get at least a six pack each, find a crate to sit on, and proceed to get drunk. We were all getting pretty well oiled when, suddenly, a heavy machine gun opened up from across-river on the south bank. I remember watching the bullets hit the hull and dent and chip the paint. The enemy gunner had elevated far too much, and he did no damage to anyone. There was a sudden rush of men to get back aboard the ship--drunks were stumbling up the brow, slowing everyone down. It was push and shove to get aboard. The quarterdeck sounded general quarters, and we stumbled to our stations. The forward gun crew on the quad-forty mount got into action first. They had the four barrels pointed straight down at the water and were shooting the hell out of the river, right in front of the ship. The captain was screaming at them on the sound-powered phone to get the guns up. So, they got the barrels pointed skyward and began shooting at outer space. The captain ordered the ship to get underway, since the VC machine-gunner had not quit trying to blast us. I think the captain and all the officers were in various stages of inebriation themselves--he had forgotten to order the anchor raised, resulting in the ship's moving and then spinning on its anchor. The ship's gunners were trying to get aimed at the south bank, but the spinning ship made that impossible, even if they had been sober.

I have no idea what the other ships in the flotilla were doing during that comedy act we staged. We finally secured from general quarters and found our way to our bunks to sleep off the drunkenness. It was another one of the off-the-wall incidents that the crew of the *Askari* experienced.

Sometime in April of that year, we were anchored upriver from Dong Tam, above Vinh Long, on an operation. It was another Sunday, but without the beer, and we were on holiday routine. That meant if we did not have to stand a watch, we could sleep in as long as we wanted. I woke up and decided to go on deck and walk around. Just as I got my eyes level with the main deck, the VC hit the whole flotilla with an intense rocket attack--fire was flying everywhere, and boats were getting hit, one after another. I saw two boats erupt in flames and pull off their moorings to get clear from other boats. We went to general quarters immediately, along with every other ship and boat in the MRF.

It was very unusual for the enemy to attack us during daylight--they evidently were in enough force, because they were standing and fighting. The Tom Green County, the fleet LST, got underway, because she was receiving the brunt of the rocket attack and took about a dozen hits. I can't remember the casualty count. She opened up on the bank, right at the river line, with her six, rapid-fire, three-inch guns. Our .40s were firing as fast as the loaders could drop in the eight-round clips. All the other ships and boats had their guns trained on the south bank, firing as fast as the machine guns would go--there were literally hundreds of guns going off. When I looked at the river bank, I saw something horrible--the VC had waited for a convoy of dozens of sampans, going to market, to get between them and us. Then they had opened up on the MRF, probably thinking we wouldn't shoot back because of the farmers being in harm's way.

Our fire was blowing sampans out of the water right along the shoreline, because the VC were level with the surface of the river, shooting at us. Trees were being splintered and blown apart from thousands of .50 caliber, 20mm, 40mm, three-inch shells, and 82mm mortar rounds. The people on the sampans were utterly destroyed, and most, if not all, of the VC were killed as well. That particular shootout went on for several minutes before it finally ceased--it was the largest attack I was ever involved in. The VC hurt us to some extent, but it never changed what we were doing and certainly never deterred us from our operations within the delta. But, it was one hell of a shoot-out.

Chapter 6

We had a section of the O1 level set up as a
movie theater, with folding chairs lined up
under a waterproof, canvas tent. There was a
popcorn machine and some kind of fake, ice
cream contraption that made something like
ice cream. The sides were covered and blacked
out, which actually worked very well for
showing movies. One night when I was sitting
there watching a flick, the roof of the tent
ripped open as a large, hot chunk of metal
crashed down right next to my chair. It was
part of the casing from a star shell that had
been shot from Dong Tam. The base would
shoot off flares and star shells whenever they
had enemy movements along the perimeter. I
was really glad I didn't get hit with that hunk of
slag.

One other time while I was on the mid-watch, I was lying on the rubberized, canvas cover of the metal, flag bag. There was almost nothing for a signalman to do on watch at night--he certainly couldn't send flashing light, not if he wanted to survive, because the snipers would have shot him full of holes. So, I was lying there, looking up at the stars, listening to the ever-present, large insects humming around the bridge. Above the flag bag was the mast, yardarm, and the twenty-four-inch searchlight, which was rarely used. Because the pilot house/conn, mast, and yardarms were behind the ship's funnel, the upper works would get coated with heavy soot. While I was staring into space, a large chunk of soot slapped into my eyes. I had no warning it was coming, so it hit me right in the pupils. The pain was intense, and I couldn't see anything. I felt my way down the ladder and woke the corpsman. He laid me down and irrigated the soot from my eyes for several minutes. Then he placed some medicine in my eyes to take away the pain and told me to stay there for the rest of my watch. His treatment was successful, but I had been very worried I would go blind from the sharp, carbon filaments in the soot.

After being aboard the *Askari* for months, I learned to stay out of trouble and keep to myself for the most part. However, between the frequent operations, lack of sleep, and added tension of snipers taking shots at us on a regular basis, it was beginning to have its effect on me. I was dealing with lousy food-- the bread was full of weevils and crunched while being chewed--and, as I previously mentioned, the drinking water was right out of the river and run through desalters. After seeing bodies floating downriver, rats swimming around, and knowing that the Mekong was nothing but a sewer all the way from China, most of us didn't relish drinking it.

One day, I noticed a couple of new replacements, kids around 19 years old, sporting black eyes, lumps, and bumps on their heads. They were not in my division, but I was concerned about them, because I suspected foul play. I asked one of them what was going on, and he told me the chief master at arms and his buddy, another chief, had beaten him shortly after he had reported aboard. Evidently, the chiefs had wanted the kids to know who was boss and not to get crosswise with them. I have hated bullies ever since experiencing their abuse as a grade school kid. I learned how to deal with them over the years—never allow them to continue their actions but deal with them quickly and forcefully. I didn't care what rank those fool chiefs were—they were hurting those kids who had no idea of what was supposed to go on. Therefore, I determined to put a stop to it.

I cornered the chief master at arms and told him I knew about his chicken-shit, abusive treatment of those kids. I made him an offer— for him to bring his buddy and his friggin', .45 pistol and meet me on the fantail that night at 2200 (10:00 p.m.). I informed him that he and his friend could beat on me, and then I was going to beat the hell out of them and throw them both into the Mekong River. Or, they could stop their twisted entertainment at the expense of mere kids, for good. I promised him I would be there right on time--and I was. I had a brass, belaying pin in each of my hands while I waited for them in the dark on the fantail, right above an easy drop into the river. Being the cowardly bullies, they were, they never showed up but they never beat up another kid again, at least while I was aboard.

My nerves, frayed from the long, pent-up frustration, finally snapped when, having moved downriver on an op, we were returning to Dong Tam to anchor. The whole flotilla had been warned by army intelligence (an oxymoron, for sure) that we were going to be ambushed somewhere in the narrows along a certain section of riverbank. This same kind of warning had been given time and time again without ever being proven true--it had been month after month of the same, old bullshit about dangerous ambush points, which kept us in a constant state of tension. Fueling my frustration was the fact that we had never been trained on the small arms needed to protect our ship from boarders--I wasn't sure how to operate the BAR, let alone practice shooting one. So, after standing out in the rain and the steaming heat for hours (and, previously, for many days), I suddenly had had enough—I sharply yelled out to the chief signalman that I was going to open fire on the next VC village we sailed by and ambush the VC before they could ambush us. He got all nervous and ran into the conn to tell the captain. Alarmed, the chief signalman pleaded with me to relinquish the gun. I flat-out refused his request and laid into him with strong, colorful language. I hotly told him where he and the friggin' Navy, the war, and the army intelligence could go. It wasn't until we had anchored that a chief gunner's mate was sent up to confiscate the BAR from me. He noted, to his relief, that there wasn't a real threat--I hadn't even cocked the gun, preventing it from firing. As for me, I had begun to come my senses and felt ridiculous. I informed the gunner's mate and my own chief that none of us had had any training on the small arms and that I wasn't coming up to the bridge anymore during night attacks and general quarters.

I wasn't the first sailor to blow up under pressure on board the *Askari*, so, funny thing-- they just sent me to my rack to sleep it off. The very next day, it was announced that anyone wishing to fire small arms could ride the Admin boat to the south bank and shoot any and all the small arms weapons they desired. I took a half dozen 30.06 BAR clips and the BAR. When we got over there, we set up some targets and proceeded to fire the BAR, M-16s, .38 revolvers, an M-60 machine gun, shotguns, and a B-40 grenade launcher--my favorites were the grenade launcher and the M-60 machine gun. The BAR I considered worthless, because it climbed right up above the target, due to recoil. But the M-60 was very accurate and really easy to shoot--I ran the whole 100-round belt without stopping. We had a great time "practicing" with the "toys" and then departed for the ship. I never went up to the bridge during a night attack again. The Captain must have thought my idea had been a good one, because, from that point on, he secured all unnecessary personnel from the bridge during night attacks. After his order, I would don my flak jacket and helmet, head for a massive lathe down in the well deck, and lie under it until we secured from GQ.

Chapter 7

The *Askari* had been ordered to transit to
Singapore and the British Kings dock for repair.
We had waited for our replacement to arrive--
another ARL, the USS *Sphinx*; then we headed
for Vung Tau and the South China Sea.

We were underway, south off of Vung Tau
close to sunset, when another ship on the
horizon began to exchange calls with us. I was
on watch and noted that the other ship used
the international call for ship-to-ship
identification. I suspected she was a Navy
vessel, whose Captain was probably thinking
we were a merchant ship. It is a regular
practice for ships to identify themselves to
each other, particularly in wartime. I was right
in the middle of sending our call sign to the
other ship, when the Officer of the Deck
ordered me to cease sending flashing light. He

was a "snipe", an engineering officer who worked below deck in the engine room. He had no idea about what I was engaged in, and I suspected he was worried he might get in trouble with the Captain. I repeatedly informed him that I had to complete the exchange of calls, according to protocol, but he wouldn't hear of it. I told him that the other ship was most likely an American warship of some kind, but he still refused to let me do my job.

The other ship was steaming in the opposite direction from us and continued to send the inquiry, "What ship? Where from? Where bound?". When his 12-inch light was out of range, the other ship's signalman resorted to using his 24-inch, search light, continuing to send the same message. The gigantic light's, blasting beam was so powerful, I had to read it through closed eyelids. We finally sailed out of visual range and into the darkness.

The "snipe" (engineering officer) knew as much about standing Officer of the Deck as I did about the engines in his space below. He should have been qualified as a line officer, but he obviously was not. Therefore, I became afraid, really afraid, of the consequences of our failure to identify ourselves. I had good reason to fear what was likely to come--I told that officer we were about to get our sorry asses blown out of the water by our own navy. He was spooked, too, but he wouldn't admit it--I could see it on his face. My friend, the quartermaster, and I worried over our situation--it wasn't good, and we were both sure we were probably going to be sunk.

There is a procedure called a "challenge" in Navy terminology and operations. It means that one ship challenges another ship to identify itself during wartime, when the challenging ship suspects the other ship to be the enemy. This is how it works: there is a safe onboard that holds challenge codes, which change every so many hours. The Captain authorizes the signalman to send the official, current, challenge code to the other ship. The challenging ship goes to general quarters, trains their guns on the other ship, and waits for the correct reply via flashing light. If the wrong reply is sent, the challenging ship opens fire on the other ship.

Well now, we hadn't even finished the regular exchange of calls to the mystery ship on the horizon, which had to look very suspicious to that navy patrol vessel. One serious mistake, due to ignorance by one officer, could get everyone killed aboard any ship that failed to maintain protocol--that we were that ship, I had no doubt.

I walked to the after part of the bridge to get away from the idiot officer of the deck. My friend, Jerry, joined me, searching the darkness off the mouth of the Mekong Delta and Vung Tau. We hadn't long to wait before we spotted red and green running lights, low down, just above the water--it was a fast-approaching airplane. Then it got "real," as they say, when its lights were turned off. I announced to Jerry, "This is it!".

Suddenly, with a great, thundering roar and a brilliant, white light illuminating our ship, a P-3 Orion, a four-engine, anti-submarine aircraft buzzed our ship, not fifty feet above the mast, and roared into the night sky. It circled around us a couple times, then headed back the way it had come.

Thankfully, not long before leaving the river, I had repainted a large, American flag on the flat top of the conn--the pilot had evidently seen it and had radioed our ship for identification. An

Orion carries bombs and depth charges--we had been that close to destruction. We had just begun our journey to Singapore, closely avoiding being blown to hell in the South China Sea. I took another giant, mental step in my disgust of the Navy and the Vietnam War. We were only just starting the fiasco of that trip to the repair dock. The journey didn't get better anytime soon.

I had already heard about Air Force F-4s attacking two ships, an Aussie destroyer, and a Navy patrol boat, off of the DMZ, in June of 1968. Four men had died in that "mistake" of "friendly fire."

When my watch was over, I headed for my bunk to get some sleep. I was pretty certain we were out of harm's way, safely on our way to the exotic port of Singapore, and there shouldn't be any problem getting there. Well, as it turned out, I was wrong in making that assumption, once again.

A new navigation officer had reported aboard the *Askari* just a couple months before we had begun our trip to the repair docks in Singapore. He was tall and lanky, with red hair and a kind of detached air about him. Working on the bridge gave me insight into most of the officers' personalities, and I invariably rubbed elbows with all of them. This character, the navigator, was about as uncoordinated as a human being could possibly get--he was constantly ramming his head into the top of the hatch in the conn or tripping over the raised section of the bottom of the hatch.

All of the signalmen, most of the radarmen and quartermasters, and the majority of officers would slide down the ladder railings from the bridge level to the next level below. We would grab both railings and kick off, keeping our feet up until we reached the lower deck--we did that multiple times a day. Many of us would also run back up the ladder without using the handrails--it was our regular routine.

Well, this one guy, whom we nicknamed "The Dork," studied those maneuvers, day in and day out until he figured he could do it, too. I was sitting on the starboard wing of the bridge, leaning on a 12-inch signal light, looking straight down the ladder at the lower deck, when "The Dork" appeared below. He hesitated a few seconds at the foot of the ladder before attempting to run up it without holding onto the railings. He had made it about halfway up, in a frenzy of feet, elbows, and knees, when it happened--his foot slipped off the metal rung, and down he went, slamming his chin onto one of the rungs. He hung there a second before completing the fiasco by tumbling to the deck in a moaning, groaning, heap. My own jaw hurt just watching that sorry performance. Over the next few weeks, I witnessed his repeated attempts to slide down the rails of the ladder, almost breaking his bones and tripping, time and again, on the hatch at the entrance to the conn. One day, a look came across his face like a light had just come on in his brain—he had come up with a "bright" idea. In an attempt to avoid tripping, he had decided to step directly onto the raised portion of the hatch, but he hadn't calculated his need to bend over, so, this time, he drove the top of his skull, with the full force of his lurch forward, into the unforgiving, steel overhead. He fell into the conn, groaning and holding his head----that move had to really smart. He bounced off the binnacle, almost crashing into the wheel while we were underway. It was much like watching a Three Stooges or an Abbot and Costello act. He was so pathetic that I had a hard time restraining my laughter whenever he arrived on the bridge.

That same "navigator" was now suddenly responsible for getting us through the South China Sea, in the dark, avoiding the islands and shoals that littered that part of the ocean— definitely a tall order for that individual. I have no idea how he had ever been promoted to Lieutenant, but he had been. We were now at his mercy and saddled with his inept performance as navigator. As darkness fell, we were making a startling, six knots, wallowing along on a course that our "navigator" had set. If I had known what was about to occur, I doubt I would have been sleeping soundly, trusting that the ship was in good hands.

My friend, Jerry, a quartermaster, was on watch, and witnessed the entire episode. Evidently, "The Dork" was standing OD while also acting as navigator during the mid-watch.

The ship was beginning to encounter some moderate seas as the old tub floundered along in the dark with him at the conn. Jerry was looking out forward when, without warning, waves began breaking all around the ship, producing white water everywhere--"the Dork" had plotted a course directly for the largest shoal in the South Pacific. I have no idea what took place on the bridge that night, but someone took control of the situation and got the *Askari* away from its likely sinking. That fool navigator was a menace, not only to himself, but to the survival of the entire ship and its crew--I heard all about it the next morning during my watch. The worst part of it was that he still wasn't finished risking the ship and her crew.

While we were approaching the Equator, some of the lifers began planning to haze those of the crew that had never crossed it before--the cowardly chief master at arms and his partner in crime thought they were about to get even with me. I got word from one of the crew that they planned to wail on me with bats and other objects when we crossed the equator. I sent a message back to them that I wasn't going be part of any kind of initiation, no matter what they had planned, and I made it perfectly clear that they had better lay off, permanently. That was the end of their attempted retribution against me.

We plodded on into some six-foot seas that were coming abeam of the ship, which caused us to take some radical port and starboard rolls. We began taking thirty-five-degree rolls to the starboard, according to the roll meter on the bridge. But, when our old tub listed to port, we took forty-five-degree rolls. The difference between the port and starboard rolls was due to the heavy, A-frame crane on the port side. We could feel it pull the ship over another ten degrees every time she rolled to that side. A forty-five-degree roll is nothing to sneeze at, so I was thankful the seas were only running about six feet. I think the old barge would have flipped if we had encountered anything like I had seen off San Francisco, while on my reserve cruise aboard the destroyer.

After several days at sea, we finally arrived off the Singapore straights--a voyage of an astounding six-hundred miles that took most of a week. A huge volume of shipping entered those straights day and night. The ships were of all sizes and traveled at different speeds, going and coming. It was a tricky place to transit, especially at night.

The Captain was in his chair on the bridge when we began to enter the narrows of the straights, making our usual six knots. I could see twelve or fifteen large ships sailing the dark waters ahead. The Captain asked the navigator what his course was--there was no answer. So, the Captain asked again about a minute later--still no response. Finally, the Captain lost his patience and began to cuss and yell about incompetent officers, slumped in his chair, and threw his hands up in the air, mumbling something under his breath.

That wasn't a good sign, as far as I was concerned. The *Askari* was rambling along in one of the most dangerous sea lanes on earth. The place was packed with traffic, red and green lights were everywhere, and lighthouses were flashing their warnings about points of rocks and dangerous shoals. "The Dork" ambled over to the back of the conn and kind of sank against the bulkhead, trying to make himself less noticeable.

Jerry, the quartermaster third class, grabbed me by the arm and said that we had to do something. So, we decided that he would plot us through the straights while I acted as expert lookout on the signal bridge. I needed to keep him informed about all ship movements, any lighthouses far ahead, and any potential collision emergencies that might arise. So, I assumed my duties with the big eye binoculars out on the wing of the signal bridge, calling out the information to Jerry, who was inside the conn. I was busy enough that I forgot my disgust and shock at the Captain, who evidently had given up on the navigator, and I just concentrated on doing my job.

We eventually reached the Kings Dock at the repair yards in the morning and tied fast to the pier. Liberty call was announced, and most of the crew changed into their whites. Jerry and I grabbed our money and made ready to depart for the fleshpots and distractions of the Far East. Many of us had not had liberty for almost a year--as for myself, I had not yet gotten the

R&R to Australia for which I had waited ten months.

There was a long line waiting to depart the ship, and we were all excited to get ashore, when the 21 MC clicked on, and a voice announced that liberty had been canceled. We were instructed to set the sea-and-anchor detail and make ready to get underway. The air erupted with cussing and yelling, the uproar of protests being loud and long. Resigned to their new orders, the crew went below decks to change out of their whites and back into dungarees. We got word that we were pulling out of Kings Dock to an anchorage about a mile away. I can only blame the Captain for the screw up. We had been ordered to unload all our ammunition onto a barge that would be pulled up to take our ordinance. The Captain should have known the regulations of the repair facility and made plans to unload before we had tied off to the pier.

An all-hands, working party was called to move the ammunition. As usual, the E-5s and above had skipped out on the all-hands part and had left it to us lowly E-4s and below to do all the work. Jerry and I got in line and began moving ammunition for a short while. We had had all of the screwing around we could take, so when the time was right, we made for the library and hid ourselves inside, behind locked doors. After the ammunition was finished being unloaded, the ship set a three-section duty, and two-thirds of the crew were embarked onto a couple boats headed for Singapore. Jerry and I were not in that first group, so we ended up standing the early morning watch, prior to the ship's getting underway for the Kings Dock.

Chapter 8

When we got ashore the next afternoon, I
followed Jerry's lead. He had been in all kinds
of Far East ports and knew the drill. He told me
the first thing to do was pick a cab driver that
would agree to meet us at a certain time and
place on the dock every day we had liberty. So,
it was, that we met Mike, who would serve as
our driver during the entire time we were in
Singapore.

Jerry instructed Mike to take us where they
served the best and cheapest beer in town.
Mike grinned, and off we went to the British
Military Club at the Raffles Hotel. They served
the brew in pints, and it was cold and tasty--
nothing like the rot-gut garbage we had been
drinking in Vietnam. A regular at the club was a
certain Aussie sailor who would open beer
bottles with his teeth, if someone bought them

for him. I bought several, waiting for his teeth to explode, but they never did.

Because the food was so terrible on board the ship, I was determined to eat a lot of fresh food while it was available. Mike hauled us around to a different international restaurant every night--we had Chinese, Russian, French, and several other types of excellent dinners. Our typical evening would consist of drinking plenty of beer at the Raffles, downing some Johnny Walker Black, Scotch whiskey, eating a great meal at an international restaurant, and then topping it off with more whiskey.

We would sometimes rent rickshaws and have races, but my favorite activity was the nightly ride through downtown Singapore at a hundred miles per hour--speed was one of those things that I yearned for after spending almost a year in Vietnam. One of us would throw Mike a twenty and tell him to hit it, and we would roar off into downtown, scattering chickens, people, and vendors in all directions. I don't know to this day how we got away with it, but we did. Afterwards, we would return to the British Military Club for more beer, and, when the night had waned, Mike would drive us to an ice cream parlor for Hot Fudge Sundaes. Later, Mike would drop us off at the ship, and we would make our way below decks to our racks and pass out.

One day, we got tanked up on beer and wandered around town on foot. We came across an outdoor market that sold local delights. There were about twenty, small, barbecued monkeys hanging in a row on hooks, staring at us with sightless eyes. Just for kicks, Jerry and I each bought one and dug in—they were surprisingly tasty. For dessert, we bought a fried banana from an outdoor vendor, who had a large shallow pan sitting over a cooking fire, filled with coal-black grease. The bananas were skewered on a bamboo stick and held in the hot grease until golden brown--they were delicious. When we finally climbed back into Mike's cab, and he drove us to the tailor district, where I bought a silk, smoking jacket for my dad, a silk robe for my mom, and sport coats, suits, and a fancy, carved, ivory chess set for myself.

We continued to partake of food and drink to excess and hit some of the seedier bars for a distraction. One particular night, the other third-class signalman on the ship accosted me in a dive we had just entered and begged me to back him up in a fight. It seemed that both he and an Australian sailor claimed to have fallen in love with the same whore. They were ready to fight over her, and this jerk wanted me to help him beat up the Aussie. I told him to drop dead, and we got back into Mike's cab and roared off into the night, laughing hysterically.

There were different groups of *Askari* sailors roaming the haunts of the town, and one particular bunch would go to the rougher parts of town to look for fights. They had a great time beating up some of the local thugs--the local tough guys were just not ready for the madmen from the Mekong. The *Askari* crew had been without a break far too long, and some of them relished street fighting--and, of course, they had to tell me about it the next day. It was pretty hard to verify their stories, but several other sailors, not involved in the fights, agreed they had indeed beat up the local tough guys. Driving fast, eating, and drinking were much more to my liking, and we kept it up until the ship was repaired and ready to pull out for the river, once again.

One day while I was on board the ship, I saw two dock workers, otherwise known as "yard birds," catch and kill a large monitor lizard-- they began cooking it on the spot. I don't know if it was worth eating or not, but having eaten a rattlesnake once, I figured a lizard might be just as tasty.

The trip back, after the short break in Singapore, was pretty much without incident-- we made Vung Tau one evening and sailed back upriver to Dong Tam the next day. The *Askari* dropped anchor off of Dong Tam, ready to resume its duties repairing the boats that had broken down or had gotten shot up. Shortly after we arrived, I got word from the yeoman in the personnel office that I was to be transferred back to the *Benewah*. The following day, I left the *Askari* for the last time. I reported aboard the *Benewah* and was notified that I was to see the XO (executive officer)—more about that later.

An interesting aside concerning another XO needs to be mentioned here. In order to get R&R to Australia, a person had to wait ten months. The wait was more than justified to me, since I wanted to go to a country that had nothing to do with the Far East, its culture, weather, stink, and turmoil. I wasn't surprised by the long wait, but I had no idea that my R&R had actually come through on time, until, one day on the way to Singapore, the XO of the *Askari* told me about it--he had taken it upon himself to cancel my long-awaited R&R to Australia. When I confronted him about it, he said he had thought I was needed on board while we were to make the transit from Vietnam to Singapore. That, of course, was a load of bullshit, and he knew it—there had been plenty of signalmen available for watch during that movement. He was an old "mustang," an officer who had begun his time as an enlisted man. He was not unusual in his abuse of power when it came to "mustangs," but he had completely screwed me over—he had stolen my one reprieve from the constant, lousy conditions, stress, and danger of being on a ship at war--a reprieve for which I had not only qualified but had patiently waited and anticipated for ten months. So, when I saw him a couple days before leaving the *Benewah* for Saigon, I just couldn't let it go without expressing exactly what I thought of him. I didn't care a whit about "getting in trouble" for cussing out that sorry sucker--I did it, and he could go where it was hot….hotter than Vietnam.

In order to reduce paperwork for the yeomen aboard the ships, it had been decided to allow the personnel that were ready for transfer back to the States to fill out their own time and date for their transfer. The rule was we could leave country on the same month we had left the United States, enroute to Vietnam. Since Vietnam was halfway around the world, its time zone was one day ahead of Pacific Time. Therefore, even though I had arrived in Danang, Vietnam, the first of September, I had left the U.S. on the 31st of August. While filling out the transfer papers, I immediately saw the advantage of using August for my transfer date, so I contacted Mike Dowling, who was aboard the *Benewah.* Mike and I had flown over from the States together and wanted to leave together, so I told him to fill out the forms just like mine. He understood what I was getting at and immediately urged me to put in for the first of August. I told him I thought that was a bit too obvious and replied, "Let's go for the fifth of August--it probably won't be noticed." I figured that three weeks early would be a fitting time to depart that hell hole and get away from the Mobile Riverine Force. We were following the letter of the law, if not the spirit. And by that point, in my experience, the spirit of anything dealing with that war just didn't matter at all.

The XO of the *Benewah* called me into his office, had me sit down, and began to go over the date I was to be transferred from the ship, in order to fly back to the States. He said something like, "If I had known earlier that you and Dowling had pulled this stunt, I would have kept you aboard for another three weeks. But since I have orders for you to fly out on the fifth, I have to comply with your ticket date—everything is already set. So here are your signed orders and ticket." I told him I had thought he might have kept me aboard if he had known about my leaving three weeks early, but I was very glad he had decided to honor the written departure date.

Later that day, Dowling and I both breathed a sigh of relief and, with wide grins, began mental separation from the MRF, just waiting for the soon-arriving day to dawn when we would fly out from the Mekong Delta to Saigon, the first leg of our return to the States.

Chapter 9

The Mobile Riverine Force weighed anchor and began the movement up to the crossover, in order to head downriver to Can Tho. There was to be another operation against the remaining VC forces threatening the air base and its facilities. After we anchored in the early afternoon, Mike and I took the first Admin boat to the Air Force base at Can Tho. We found the enlisted men's club and ordered hamburgers and beer. Being at an Air Force facility meant it was much more comfortable and hospitable than the army-navy base at Dong Tam. The hamburgers tasted almost like the ones back home, the beer was not rotten, and the place was clean and neat. There was a rack of civilian clothes for sale, so I bought a short-sleeve shirt--the shirt, I might add, that I wore from Saigon to Sacramento and which I kept for over forty years. I flew to the States in civilian clothes--it felt really good.

After a few hours of sitting in the EM club, we got the call to board a hop to Ton Son Nhat, Saigon--our ride was a C-130. We walked up its rear ramp into the cargo hold, which, to our surprise, was crowded with Vietnamese women, their goats and chickens, babies, and whatever else they were carrying. I had no idea what they were doing in there, but the ride was our ticket to get out of the delta, so we gladly shared the dung-covered floor with them and their animals. We sat on the steel deck of the plane and held onto a rope-net to keep from sliding or being flung around during the rough flight.

We were coming into Saigon in the pitch blackness of a monsoon rainstorm. It was a fitting end to a year of strange events, at least so I thought, as we touched down and taxied to a halt. We exited the cargo hold and looked for a taxi.

My only previous experience with Saigon had been the night I had spent at the army transit barracks. I knew for certain that I wasn't going to spend three days in that rotten pit, waiting for my flight home. The other alternative was to stay in the downtown Victoria Hotel. Having to pay for my own lodging was worth it, in order to avoid the transit barracks.

A cab pulled up in the driving rain, and we quickly hopped in. We both sat in the back seat, Mike on the right side and myself behind the driver, whom I instructed to go to the hotel. The only thing I knew about the Victoria Hotel was that it was a white, ten-story building, located in the middle of downtown Saigon. The driver pulled out of the airport, made a turn, and proceeded towards what we thought was downtown. It was some time before I noticed, through the driving rain, that it was getting darker, rather than lighter, like a downtown area should be. I mentioned that fact to Mike, and he got scared. It was completely dark when we pulled into a side road and stopped at a gate. We both noticed a huge, old, wooden structure in the dim light, through the sheets of pelting rain. Mike and I had heard about this place--it was an ancient, French race track, built out of wood, located at the far outskirts of the city. It was also one of the suspected hold-out locations of the remaining VC forces around Saigon. The devious cab driver was planning to take us for our last ride--one that would end in our deaths.

As I have mentioned before, I was on my own in country—basically, out of sight and out of mind, as far as the military was concerned. Mike and I had no guns, and, in effect, were nothing but tourists awaiting our fate. If something were to happen to us, we would not be missed for days, if then.

Sometime earlier on board the *Askari*, I had come across a Marine, fighting knife, a KA-BAR, which was first issued to the Marines in 1942 and saw much use in the following years. Its hardened, carbon steel, was rated 55 to 56 on the scale of hardness and ease of sharpening. It had a seven-inch blade with a large blood groove--a solid tang that went all the way through the leather-wrapped handle. To enhance the grip when wet or bloody, there were grooves cut around the tang in the handle. This was a large, no-nonsense fighting tool, so I was extremely glad and somewhat relieved as I glanced down at it, strapped onto my right hip, that fateful night in the cab. Mike leaned over to me, when he figured out what was going on, and asked me in a subdued voice what we were going to do. I emphatically replied we were going to turn around immediately and return to the hotel. He hadn't noticed the KA-BAR until I pulled it out of its sheaf.

With a combination of fear and resolve, I quickly leaned forward and put the sharp, wide blade against the driver's throat. He flinched when he felt the cold, unforgiving steel press against his throat. I informed him, in menacing tones, that he was a rotten son of a bitch and that he was going to turn around right then, or I was going to cut his friggin' head off. A KA-BAR can be a very convincing tool when there is a desperate, enraged sailor holding it at one's throat along with a muscular forearm encircling the head. The VC driver slammed on the brakes, came to an abrupt halt, hastily backed up, and urgently sped in the direction of the hotel. I kept reminding him, with an edgy voice through clenched teeth, that I would cut off his head if he tried anything, anything at all, except to drive us to the Victoria Hotel. During the tense trip there, I had conflicting thoughts as to whether I should cut him or not--he had probably done this very thing before, and it was highly likely he would do it again. But, I also reasoned that if I arrived at the hotel covered in his blood with his dead body in the cab, I would have to explain myself to the MPs or SPs. That could easily translate into a delay of our departure, and I was damned sure I didn't want any delays in getting out of that country. So, against my better judgment, when we got to the hotel, I reluctantly let the guilty, conniving driver go. To this day, I often think back on that eerie experience and sincerely hope no other unsuspecting serviceman was subsequently given a final cab ride to the Plu Tho Race Track.

We entered the hotel, got a room, and decided to head for the tenth floor to get some food. There was a regular restaurant on the top level, so we got a table and ordered something, I don't remember what. Circulating amongst the tables were quite a number of beautiful women, who looked to be a mixture of Vietnamese and French. A few were very pretty and wore classy clothes, fancy hairstyles, and tasteful makeup. They were all young, spoke good English, and were polite and friendly. I suspected they were prostitutes, and it wasn't long before I was certain. We were having our first, after-dinner whiskey when a couple of them asked if they could sit at our table. We replied, "Sure, have a seat," but we let them know we were not going to buy them drinks or anything else. We told them we were on our way home, period, and they would be wasting their time with us--they should concentrate on other guys in the room. The girls took my advice and floated off towards some other, likely-looking prospects. I ordered another whiskey, and we proceeded to get drunk. One of the other guys at the table volunteered to buy us bottles at a PX across the street. I had him bring me a fifth of Scotch and proceeded to drink the whole bottle. We hung out for a couple hours, drinking and talking about going home. No one talked about the war or their experiences in it. I was dangerously drunk and ended up with alcohol poisoning. We had barely returned to our room before I became violently sick, all over the room. In fact, we had to get another room, because I had messed up the first one so badly.

For the next two days, we ate in that restaurant, morning, noon, and night. For breakfast, they served duck eggs with very dark yokes, something I had never had before. The whores even circulated at breakfast. We continued to eat and drink with the other soldiers and sailors and waited for our flight. On our second night, a particularly beautiful woman came up to our table during dinner. She sat down and made a proposition to me-- she had been watching me and wanted to go to bed with me. She said it would be at only half the going rate. I told her I wasn't interested and she was wasting her time. Then she changed her proposal and said it would cost nothing--she was insistent that we head for my room. But, I begged off and wished her well, and she finally left the table.

The last night there, Mike and I decided to venture out to a restaurant very close to the hotel. In fact, it was just around the corner from the front door. We had been warned that it was unsafe to roam the streets of Saigon—there were still VC driving around on motor bikes and tossing grenades at Americans. But we had had it, as far as the scene in the hotel restaurant went, so we decided to take the chance and go out for dinner.

The place was called the Two Crabs, well known for excellent crab dinners. We walked around the corner and entered the restaurant. I know what crabs feed on, and the idea that they were eating every kind of dead thing in the Saigon River wasn't lost on us. But, we were in the mood for something different, so we ordered crab. In fact, I ordered two crab dinners with all the fixings. During the course of the meal, I noticed some thin strips of dried, red pepper in a small, shallow bowl sitting on the table. I could sense that the peppers were really hot, but I just had to try one. Now, I like hot food--I use a lot of Tabasco sauce on much of my food as a regular enhancer. But, these peppers, whatever they were, were hot beyond anything I have ever tasted. I just touched one to my tongue, and it was immediately on fire. I ate a couple mouthfuls of sugar, but I still had a hard time getting rid of the heat. They were actually "unbelievable,"--as much as that word is over-used, it fit the experience to a tee.

The morning came for our departure, and we caught a cab for the airport, with an important stop in between. When I had left the *Askari*, the yeoman had told me they had lost my shot card, the record of all the immunizations I had

had to date. My shots were up to date, but they couldn't provide me with the records. So, it was my responsibility to get all the shots necessary to leave country. We drove to a large Quonset hut hospital and asked for the way to the dispensary. Someone told us that it closed at noon and wouldn't be open until after one. I needed to be at the airport by one in order to check in and get aboard the flight out of country, and the dispensary was all the way on the other side of the facility. Mike and I began to run as hard as we could go. We had about five minutes left before noon, when we rushed into the room and saw a line twenty-men long. I couldn't wait--the window would close, and I would miss my flight. So, there was nothing to do but cut to the front of the line and shout out that I needed all the shots so that I could make a flight--the corpsman understood. He had me bare both arms and let me have it with the needle guns—there must have been over a dozen different inoculations included in that barrage. He filled out the shot card, I thanked him and the other guys in line, and ran for the exit and the waiting cab at the other end of the compound. We hustled to the terminal to check in and waited for our airplane.

The terminal had been shot to hell during the fighting of Tet. There were all kinds of bullet pockmarks in the walls and some large holes that were probably caused by rockets--it wasn't a comfortable place to await our turn to take off. The VC were supposedly still active at the approaches to the runways and were said to randomly shoot .50 caliber machine guns at the bellies of departing aircraft. That was something that many of us dreaded--the idea of getting shot out of the sky on departure was the last thing we wanted to consider.

When it was finally time to go through customs, I was wearing my civilian clothes. My sea bag was packed, and I was more than ready to depart. The customs officer made a little speech to all of us when we approached the tables that we had to pass in order to exit the terminal. He basically told us that if we had something in our possession that we had not come into country with, we could put it on the table, and no questions would be asked. But, if we didn't declare everything, we might be detained, and we would probably miss our flight--that was enough for me. I reached into the sea bag and fished out the KA-BAR--I wanted to do nothing that would detain me. I hated to leave it there, because it had literally saved my life and that of Mike's, but keepsakes at a time like that are unimportant. I tossed it onto the table and walked to the exit.

I have never seen so many aircraft lined up, waiting to leave an airport. Our airplane was a Banff Airlines 707. There were civilian airplanes and many different kinds of military aircraft, nose to tail for at least a mile, waiting to depart. We got in the line, eventually turned from the taxi way, and rumbled down the runway and into the air. We cleared the airspace around Saigon, didn't have trouble with any would-be snipers, and set a course for Yokota Air Force base, Japan. It was to be a five-hour flight to our stop-over in Japan.

I could feel the tension go out of my body when we cleared the coastline of Vietnam and noticed the other passengers were relieved, too, with the same body language. Our route would take us east of Hainan Island, China, across part of the East China Sea to our first stop. We were cruising at forty thousand feet when the pilot came on the intercom and announced we were beginning to fly over a typhoon. The stewardesses were in the middle of serving us a meal, when the mood turned. Suddenly, we were thrust back into a state of fear-of-dying on the way home.

The airplane fell out of the sky--it wasn't any longer flying, but dropping like a rock. We descended for what seemed like a very long time, maybe thirty seconds, before hitting bottom, hard. The food had been coming up off our plates, and the liquid in the drinks was two and a half feet above our heads--we were trying to catch it in our cups and glasses. The stewardesses were slammed to the floor when we hit, and all manner of food and drink flew around the cabin and drenched us. I was seated between two black guys who had been drinking milk while I had coffee--they turned white, and I turned brown when our beverages splashed into our faces. Everything was a mess, including emotions--I couldn't believe I had finally gotten out of that smelly hell hole, only to be in danger of crashing into the sea. I was worried the wings might shear off from the hard impact. We endured a rough ride for several minutes, and then we finally cleared the hurricane's wrath. No one was interested in drinking or eating food after that, even if there had been some left that hadn't hit the floor.

We landed in Yokota, somewhat the worse for wear with stained clothes, but happy to be on the ground after the typhoon experience. I had determined not to act the fool when I saw the new guys headed for Vietnam, like those other seasoned sailors had acted towards me a year before. I smiled at them and said, "Hi," and left them to their misery. We were there about an hour or so to gas up before heading across the pond for home.

It was a twelve-hour flight to Travis Air Force Base, outside of Sacramento, California. Most of us slept a good part of the way. Eventually, I woke up and was watching out the windows, paying attention to the view, when the pilot switched on the intercom to say, "If you look out the windows on the left side of the plane, you can see the coast of California in the distance." Everyone looked, and some of us cheered and some of us wept and some of us clapped, but we all breathed a collective sigh of relief. Home was in sight, and we had made it. That feeling is hard to describe, but it was deep and strong. The approach to the runway was long, but finally the wheels touched down, and the airplane braked to a stop and turned for the taxiway. When we pulled up to the terminal, I could see a lot of people lined up against the fence, cheering and waving out a welcome. When my feet hit the tarmac, I jumped up and down gleefully, three times, before heading to the gate. I was welcomed by several strangers, patting me on the back and saying, "Hi," and, "God bless you," and, "Welcome home, boy." It felt so good, and I will always remember the welcome by those concerned, friendly, complete strangers.

After going through customs again, I walked out front and located a

Greyhound bus that was headed for the San Francisco airport. There was a really friendly driver seated at the wheel. We loaded up our bags, and he closed the door and pulled out. He flipped on the mike and told us to relax, that he was going to get us to the airport in record time. That Greyhound lived up to its name, and we fairly flew down the freeway.

I intended to fly to Los Angeles on PSA Airlines, because, at that time, they flew every hour, on the hour, between Los Angeles and San Francisco. They were famous for flying 727s with good-looking stewardesses wearing mini-skirts. I was eager to get a look at those legs and faces--American girls in American clothes, on American airplanes, in America.

I called home from a phone booth in the airport to alert my family that I was in San Francisco. My folks were overjoyed that I was back, and they mentioned they had, just that day, received my letter explaining I would be arriving on the fifth of August. They were taken totally by surprise to find that I was on my way home, the same day they had received my letter. They would have to hustle, but they assured me they would be at the airport when I arrived in LA. I went into the men's room and changed into my uniform whites for the trip to Los Angeles. The flight down was a short hour; then we were there. It was great to see Mom and Dad and my two sisters standing with the many others awaiting their sons' arrivals back from the war, but I stopped walking towards them and hesitated for a few seconds before continuing on. I realized that I was a different person from the one they had seen off a year before, and I wasn't sure what to do, what to say, or how to act--the delay was brief, but significant. I moved forward and trusted that our family connection would carry us through the initial strangeness I had felt. They welcomed me with love and open arms.

We got into the car and made our way back home to PV (Palos Verdes). My family had set up a large banner in the front yard, welcoming me home—it felt really good. We talked and visited for a while and then headed off to bed. Glad to be back in my own room, I petted my dog and then sacked out. Early in the morning, I got up and walked outside to look at the sea, smell the salt air, untainted from the stink of the tropics, and to just watch normal people drive off to work. While standing there in the yard, a garbage truck came down the road and backfired near me--I found myself on the ground, waiting for incoming, before I realized what had just happened. My heart was racing, but I calmed down quickly enough and thanked God it was just the backfire from a garbage truck. I was home, not in a far-off war zone, and I knew it would all be OK.

Chapter 10

I had a thirty-day leave before I was to report to the AKA, USS *Union*, in San Diego, so my family decided to go on a trip. My Dad rented a Clark Cortez motorhome, and we headed off to Idaho to do some fishing. On the way, we stopped in Virginia City, Nevada, where we touristed it up. Dad and I had beers at the Bucket of Blood Saloon and other watering holes; then we pulled out for the mountains of Idaho. I chose to drive, and my family had to insist that I slow down. I guess the open road and the freedom of tooling across Nevada after being on the ship for a year caused me to be a bit careless. We fooled around the Payette River country, camped at Red Fish Lake, and fished the Big Wood River above Sun Valley--I saw my first river otters while fly-fishing on the Wood. We also fished Silver Creek, famous even at that time. I had a hard time fly-casting because of the tulles surrounding the section of the creek we were fishing, but I did catch some trout on dry flies. My dad and sisters were not having much luck, so we stopped at a little store in Picabo and bought night crawlers--you couldn't do that now on Silver Creek, even if you owned the place, but it was allowable back then, in 1968. We caught some beautiful rainbows up to 19 inches. They had magenta-red sides, black backs, and green and white bellies. We took a limit with us to eat when we departed the following day for California.

My leave flew by all too quickly, and I soon found myself reporting aboard the USS *Union*. It was an attack cargo ship that had recently returned from a Westpac (Western Pacific) cruise off the coast of Vietnam. The ship was tied up to one of the destroyer piers. Three-section duty was set, with two-thirds of the crew on liberty at any one time. It turned out to be a squared-away ship. The chief signalman was a good guy who knew how things worked, and I was glad to be on board an actual ocean-going vessel. But the down side of the whole thing was the ship was going to begin sea trials in preparation for departing for Westpac within a couple of months--my heart sank. That the ship was going back to Vietnam and Southeast Asia was all I could think about, and it made me depressed. I hated the thought of getting anywhere close to those sorry shores, so there began a series of ideas running through my mind. I seriously considered going absent without leave, AWOL--but, much to my surprise, my dilemma was solved in just a few days.

Lyndon Johnson, one of the absolutely worst presidents this country has ever had the misfortune to endure, was so pressed by the unpopularity of the Vietnam War that he declared anyone having served in country for a year would get an early out. That announcement fell on welcoming ears across the whole of the real, actual, Vietnam Vets. There have been some weird claims made by people who never were in country that they were Vietnam Vets--it seems that posers never cease.

I had been scheduled to be separated from active duty the first of June, 1969--my new separation date was then set for October 31, 1968. No one was happier, anywhere, than I was--it meant that I could enroll in college for the spring semester. I could make plans to finish up with a degree that would ready me for a career in the National Park Service.

The relaxed, three-section duty aboard the *Union* allowed me to spend two days at home and one day aboard ship. I bought a 1964, Ford Econoline van, which my dad and I began to convert into a camper. I intended to make a month-long ski trip with my friend, Glenn

Sexton, who was also a Vietnam Vet. We were to be joined by another friend, Danny Reed, for the first week of the trip. In the meantime, I had my duties to perform aboard the *Union*.

When on duty, I kept the bridge clean and made sure I was on it during the day. There was actually nothing to do while we were in port, so I usually raised the November flag on the yardarm and set about reading a book while getting a tan on the signal bridge. The November flag meant there was no visual watch--that way no one would call me up with their 12-inch, signal light to just shoot the breeze, out of boredom. It was a common thing to do when in port. One day, I was lying on a towel with the November flag flying, getting some rays, when I heard footsteps and figured my chief was on the bridge. It turned out to be a chief radioman walking around my space. He accosted me and demanded to know what I was doing. I told him the obvious, pointed out the flag on the yardarm, and asked him what he wanted. He was upset, because I was in my swimming trunks, reading a book, with the November flag waving proudly off the yardarm. So, he lit into me--it was all bullshit, and we both knew it. If, and it was a very big "if," we actually needed to pull out from the pier, I was awake, on the bridge, and ready to do my duty. Otherwise, I asked him just what the hell he was doing, poking around the signal bridge as a radioman. He didn't take that too well, and neither did I. Not very long after that, my own chief showed up. It was likely that the radioman weenie had called him at home.

My chief said that, in order to keep the peace in the chiefs' quarters, he had to discipline me in some way. The chief radioman had threatened to report me to the captain, which I wouldn't mind--I knew the captain would probably forget the whole thing. But, because I liked my chief and did not want to cause him anymore grief, I told him to go ahead with the discipline. I persuaded him to agree to tell that radio puke to stay off the signal bridge, and he was glad to relay the message--he didn't like that character any more than I did. It turned out I had to clean up the chief petty officers' lounge, clean the toilets, empty and clean up all the ash trays, and buff the floor, which was no big deal. I got it all done, left the ship, and flew home that night. I always flew on PSA, since they had flights leaving San Diego for LA every thirty minutes.

The 31st of October came none too soon, and I received my separation orders from active duty in the Navy, back into civilian life. Shortly after the separation, I had to go to the Naval Reserve Center in downtown LA to sign up for my remaining reserve duty time. I was supposed to receive my discharge in April of 1972, leaving a significant amount of reserve time. Before active duty, I had attended a naval reserve unit that met once a week, for sixteen months, but the unit had been disbanded sometime after I had gone on active duty.

The chief petty officer at the downtown Naval Reserve Center gave me some choices for future reserve duty. One of the choices was to attend once-a-month meetings, followed by a two-week cruise once a year--I told him, "No." The next was to skip any meetings during the year but go on a cruise for six weeks once a year--I definitely told him, "No," on that little plan. I considered it almost as bad as being back on active duty, and I told him so. The last option was to have my name placed in the Naval Reserve Man Power pool in Bainbridge, Maryland. It would extend my discharge date by six years, and, if an actual war or large national emergency occurred, I could possibly be put back on active duty for the duration-- that was the one I chose. There were no meetings, no cruises, and no contact with anyone in the service--my kind of option. Subsequently, I never heard from anyone in the Naval Reserve again. And, much to my relief and complete surprise, my discharge certificate arrived soon after my original discharge date of April, 1972. They had evidently dropped the Naval Manpower Pool agreement. Therefore, I was free from any further commitments to the Navy.

There may have been some kind realization that those of us who had served in country during that war were not likely to be good choices to call back up. I do not know, and I have never explored that idea. But, whatever happened, it served to make me realize that the country may have wanted to put the Vietnam War experience, and all of those who had participated in it, out of its collective mind.

It was fashionable in Hollywood for a while to portray Vietnam Vets as drugged-out, baby-killers--losers that were the scum of the earth. They were portrayed as having long, greasy hair, wearing camo gear, holding eccentric ideas, being on the wrong side of the law, being violent bullies or mystical hippies, and set on self-destruction. They were pictured as drags on society that should be avoided, but the truth is just the opposite, which is not surprising, considering Hollywood never gets it right. Between believing what Hollywood portrays and what the news media says, we have a classic case of being exactly opposite of the truth.

A major study was completed by a Vietnam Vet, some years back, that proved the majority of vets were just the opposite of the myth created by the media. According to his statistics, Vietnam Veterans were much more likely than the average civilian to have started their own businesses, to have stable marriages, to have completed college, to have happy families, and to have been successful in whatever careers they had chosen.

Chapter 11

The lesson I have learned from the war is that it is crucial to understand that this country has been manipulated by the liars of the deep state, and all of its various minions, to engage in wars justified by false flag attacks. We have been the military arm of the globalists, and it has caused untold death and destruction. Their plan of action has served the central bankers, multi-national corporations, and the globalist plotters in their scheme to destroy the United States and push us into their one-world government. It is very important to pay close attention whenever events occur that have an all-too-easy explanation from the fake media and government elites.

Lyndon Johnson was a war criminal, along with his Secretary of Defense, Robert McNamara. They lied about how the North Vietnamese had attacked us in the Gulf of Tonkin. They lied about what our purpose was in the war. They lied about winning the war. They lied about the supposed threat from a communist conspiracy to destroy the United States--North Vietnam was never a threat to the United States. And, they lied for personal gain. They are responsible for upwards of two million, dead Vietnamese, for the death of almost sixty-thousand Americans, and for the near-destruction of the United States itself. Who knows what lasting carnage they caused to the very many wounded who were sent home missing parts of themselves?

The same, elite cabal that John Kennedy described in his famous 1961 speech, before they blew his brains out, still pushes to control us, and, in fact, the whole world. The lies are insidious, and the results are grim. It should behoove every American to actually learn from the past and apply it to the present. If not, well then, we may be facing a much more dangerous future than just another globalist, elitist war.

Please read the information contained in the appendix--it supports my above accusations. The information was finally released after forty years of being kept from the public. It should open your eyes to the duplicity of the evil man that was once president of the United States-- Johnson was the worst president that this country has suffered since Woodrow Wilson signed the Federal Reserve Act, instituted the illegal income tax, and plunged the United States into World War I--a war, by the way, that he had pledged to keep us out of. Sound familiar? Johnson claimed that Barry Goldwater would get us into a nuclear war with the Russians if he was elected in 1964. Instead, Johnson gave us Vietnam.

Epilogue

In January of 1969, I re-entered college and, two years later, graduated from Northern Arizona University with a Bachelor's of Science degree in Recreation and Land Management. It was specifically designed for a career in the National Park Service as a Park Ranger or Park Historian. The year I graduated, I visited Grand Canyon National Park to speak with one of the rangers. At that time, I had already worked one season for Sequoia & Kings Canyon National Parks as a back-country ranger, a position I held for five summer seasons.

The ranger at Grand Canyon told me I had all of the qualities they were looking for--a veteran's preference, a degree in a Park Service-related major, seasonal experience, and obvious interest in the job. But, he stated that I would never be hired as a permanent employee, because I was not a minority or a female. Affirmative action was the ruling doctrine of the day, and he was correct--I never got a permanent job there. Eventually, I gave up on the idea of working for the Park Service, and I became a carpenter.

Considering my experience in Vietnam, I now realize that I had actually come away with some positive lessons, which I have applied throughout my life. Looking back, I can see that having to fend for myself that year in country gave me the ability to pursue my future with little reliance upon conventional means of employment. It also enabled me make decisions about what was important for the times I lived through, and it fanned the fires of an independent spirit.

I now understand that some of those events on the river helped steel me for things I was to experience in subsequent years. I certainly became a much better college student. Prior to the war I had been a C student at a local, junior college, but after I returned, I finished my last two, college years at Northern Arizona University with an A-minus. I was probably a better back-country ranger because of it, and I certainly became a better provider for my family through the economic uncertainties of a construction career. My wife and I have experienced the common boom-and-bust economics of being dependent upon construction for a living. We have moved from California to Colorado, to Montana, to California, and back to Montana. It turned out to have been worth all of the stress and uncertainty, because we dearly love living in the mountains, and we especially love Montana.

Additionally, I have concluded that it is important to stay informed about the times and to question the pronouncements of the news media, the purveyors of lies and myths fed to the public for their consumption.

A very important word about the year from August, 1967, to August, 1968. I am certain that I came through my time over there because of the many people praying for me-- my folks and family being foremost. I in no way discount the influence of the mighty hand of God in safely bringing me home. I am grateful to Him for his providential protection throughout my entire life and for His Spirit that assures me I am one of His.

Credit is due the repair division of the USS *Askari*. The skill and tenacity of the shipfitters, welders, and mechanics aboard the ship in the years it plied the muddy water of the Mekong River system was outstanding. Their ability and their accomplishment, in large measure, assured the success of the MRF in the delta. During the time I happened to be aboard, the *Askari* was awarded two, Navy Commendation medals and a Presidential Unit Citation. The *Askari* went on to achieve more praise and commendation before she was eventually given over to the South Vietnamese. The repair division was known as the most experienced and competent within the war zone. Those people could actually do things that others were incapable of, and because of their dedication, the results they achieved were exceptional.

Appendix

The following information is taken directly from an article entitled "The Truth About Tonkin" from the Naval History Magazine, February, 2008, Volume 22, Number I, by Lieutenant Commander Pat Paterson, a foreign area officer and former history instructor at the U.S. Naval Academy.

Here is the link for the article: https://www.usni.org/magazines/navalhistory/2008-02/truth-about-tonkin.

On page 5 of this article we pick up the story.

> Back on board the *Ticonderoga*, Commander Stockdale had been ordered to prepare to launch an air strike against the North Vietnamese targets for their "attacks" of the previous evening. Unlike Captain Herrick,

Stockdale had no doubt about what had happened: "We were about to launch a war under false pretenses, in the face of the on-scene military commander's advice to the contrary." [19] Despite his reservations, Stockdale led a strike of 18 aircraft against an oil storage facility at Vinh, located just inland of where the alleged attacks on the *Maddox* and *Turner Joy* had occurred. Although the raid was successful (the oil depot was completely destroyed and 33 of 35 vessels were hit), two American aircraft were shot down; one pilot was killed and the second captured. [20]

On 7 August, Congress, with near unanimity, approved the Gulf of Tonkin Resolution, which President Johnson signed into law three days later. Requested by Johnson, the resolution authorized the chief executive to "take all necessary measures to repel any armed attack against the forces of the United States and to prevent further aggression." No approval or oversight of military force was required by Congress, essentially eliminating the system of checks and balances so fundamental to the U.S. Constitution. On hearing of the authorization's passage by both houses of Congress, the delighted President remarked that the resolution "was like Grandma's nightshirt. It covers everything." [21]

Analysis of the Evidence

Historians have long suspected that the second attack in the Gulf of Tonkin never occurred and that the resolution was based on faulty evidence. But no declassified information had suggested that McNamara, Johnson, or anyone else in the decision-making process had intentionally misinterpreted the intelligence concerning the 4 August incident. More than 40 years after the events, that all changed with the release of the nearly 200 documents related to the Gulf of Tonkin incident and transcripts from the Johnson Library.

These new documents and tapes reveal what historians could not prove: There was not a second attack on U.S. Navy ships in the Tonkin Gulf in early August 1964. Furthermore, the evidence suggests a disturbing and deliberate attempt by Secretary of Defense McNamara to distort the evidence and mislead Congress.

Among the most revealing documents is a study of the Gulf of Tonkin incidents by NSA historian Robert J. Hanyok. Titled "Skunks, Bogies, Silent Hounds, and the Flying Fish: The Gulf of Tonkin Mystery, 2-4 August 1964," it had been published in the classified Cryptological Quarterly in early 2001. Hanyok conducted a comprehensive analysis of SIGINT records from the nights of the attacks and concluded that there was indeed an attack on 2 August but the attack on the 4th did not occur, despite claims to the contrary by President Johnson and Secretary McNamara. According to John Prados of the independent National Security Archive, Hanyok asserted that faulty signals intelligence became "vital evidence of a second attack and [Johnson and McNamara] used this claim to support retaliatory air strikes and to buttress the administration's request for a Congressional resolution that would give the White House freedom of action in Vietnam." [22]

Almost 90 percent of the SIGINT intercepts that would have provided a conflicting account were kept out of the reports sent to the Pentagon and White House. Additionally, messages that were forwarded contained "severe analytic errors, unexplained translation changes, and the conjunction of two messages into one translation." Other vital intercepts mysteriously disappeared. Hanyok claimed that "The overwhelming body of reports, if used, would have told the story that no attack occurred." [23]

The historian also concluded that some of the signals intercepted during the nights of 2 and 4 August were falsified to support the retaliatory attacks. Moreover, some intercepts were altered to show different receipt times, and other evidence was cherry picked to deliberately distort the truth. According to Hanyok, "SIGINT information was presented in such a manner as to preclude responsible decision makers in the Johnson Administration from having the complete and objective narrative of events of 04 August 1964." [24]

And what about the North Vietnamese battle report that seemed to provide irrefutable confirmation of the attack? On further examination, it was found to be referring to the 2 August attacks against the Maddox but had been routinely transmitted in a follow-up report during the second "attack." The North Vietnamese were oblivious to the confusion it would generate.

What should have stood out to the U.S. leadership collecting all the data of these attacks was that, with the exception of the battle report, no other SIGINT "chatter" was detected during the attacks on 4 August. In contrast, during the 2 August attack NSA listening posts monitored VHF communications between North Vietnamese vessels, HF communications between higher headquarters in Hanoi and the boats, and communication relays to the regional naval station. None of these communications occurred on the night of 4 August.

The Defense Secretary's Role

Subsequently, Secretary McNamara intentionally misled Congress and the public about his knowledge of and the nature of the 34A operations, which surely would have been perceived as the actual cause for the 2 August attack on the *Maddox* and the apparent attack on the 4th. On 6 August, when called before a joint session of the Senate Foreign Relations and Armed Services committees to testify about the incident, McNamara eluded the questioning of Senator Wayne Morse (D-OR) when he asked specifically whether the 34A operations may have provoked the North Vietnamese response. McNamara instead declared that "our Navy played absolutely no part in, was not associated with, was not aware of, any South

Vietnamese actions, if there were any." [25]

Later that day, Secretary McNamara lied when he denied knowledge of the provocative 34A patrols at a Pentagon news conference. When asked by a reporter if he knew of any confrontations between the South and North Vietnamese navies, he responded: "No, none that I know of. . . . [T]hey operate on their own. They are part of the South Vietnamese Navy . . . operating in the coastal waters, inspecting suspicious incoming junks, seeking to deter and prevent the infiltration of both men and material." Another reporter pressed the issue, "Do these [patrol boats] go north, into North Vietnamese waters?" McNamara again eluded the question, "They have advanced closer and closer to the 17th parallel, and in some cases, I think they have moved beyond that in an effort to stop the infiltration closer to the point of origin." [26]

In reality, McNamara knew full well that the 34A attacks had probably provoked the 2 August attacks on the Maddox. On an audio tape from the Johnson Library declassified in December 2005, he admitted to the President the morning after the attacks that the two events were almost certainly connected:

And I think I should also, or we should also at that time, Mr. President, explain this OPLAN 34-A, these covert operations. There's no question but what that had bearing on it. On Friday night, as you probably know, we had four TP [sic] boats from [South] Vietnam, manned by [South] Vietnamese or other nationals, attack two islands, and we expended, oh, 1,000 rounds of ammunition of one kind or another against them. We probably shot up a radar station and a few other miscellaneous buildings. And following 24 hours after that with this destroyer in the same area undoubtedly led them to connect the two events. . . ." [27]

Intelligence officials realized the obvious. When President Johnson asked during a 4 August meeting of the National Security Council, "Do they want a war by attacking our ships in the middle of the Gulf of Tonkin?" CIA Director John McCone answered matter-of-factly, "No, the North Vietnamese are reacting defensively to our attacks on their offshore islands . . . the attack is a signal to us that the North Vietnamese have the will and determination to continue the war." [28]

Johnson himself apparently had his own doubts about what happened in the Gulf on 4 August. A few days after the

Tonkin Gulf Resolution was passed, he commented, "Hell, those damn, stupid sailors were just shooting at flying fish." [29]

Can the omission of evidence by McNamara be forgiven? Within time, the conflict in Vietnam would likely have occurred anyway, given the *POLITICAL and military events already in motion. However, the retaliatory attack of 5 August marked the United States' first overt military action against the North Vietnamese and the most serious escalation up to that date. The Tonkin Gulf Resolution, essentially unchallenged by a Congress that believed it was an appropriate response to unprovoked, aggressive, and deliberate attacks on U.S. vessels on the high seas, would open the floodgates for direct American military involvement in Vietnam. McNamara's intentional distortion of events prevented Congress from providing the civilian oversight of military matters so fundamental to the congressional charter. (*My emphasis on POLITICAL)

Some historians do not let the Johnson administration off so easily. Army Colonel H. R. McMaster, author of the highly acclaimed 1997 book Dereliction of Duty, accused Johnson and McNamara of outright deception:

To enhance his chances for election, [Johnson] and McNamara deceived the American people and Congress about events and the nature of the American commitment in Vietnam. They used a questionable report of a North Vietnamese attack on American naval vessels to justify the president's policy to the electorate and to defuse Republican senator and presidential candidate Barry Goldwater's charges that Lyndon Johnson was irresolute and "soft" in the foreign policy arena. [30]

For his part, McNamara never admitted his mistakes. In his award-winning 2003 video memoirs Fog of War, he remained unapologetic and even bragged of his ability to deceive: "I learned early on never answer the question that is asked of you. Answer the question that you wish had been asked of you. And quite frankly, I follow that rule. It's a very good rule." [31]

Afterword

The Tolstoy statement that "...history would be a wonderful thing, if only it were true..." could not be more appropriate concerning the incredibly long list of lies and deceptions foisted upon the American people. The wars that our country have been led into, by those who stand to profit monetarily and politically, have led to military and financial debacles of the worst kind. The carnage wreaked upon our citizens and those others in the world we have invaded or attacked has been enormous.

Maybe it is time to finally put a halt to the adventurism of the elite and ultra-rich globalists, who profit from our pain and suffering. Maybe it is time to actually return to representative government. Maybe it is time to completely ignore the siren sound of the war drums and absolutely refuse to engage in those "other guys' wars." The globalists and deep-state plotters have a dismal record of destruction to ultimately answer for. I have come to the conclusion that I want nothing to do with the New World Order—neither their rules, their lies, nor their wars. I hope President Trump and the patriots are successful in destroying the deep-state traitors within the United States. We will all be better for it—may he and those with him succeed.

"Where We Go One We Go All."

Gary Reichert, Montana, 2019

Made in the USA
Monee, IL
29 December 2023

50471879R00102